MW01101493

TOUCHSTONES VOLUME II

TEACHER'S GUIDE

by

Howard Zeiderman

Published by

TOUCHSTONES
DISCUSSION PROJECT

About the Touchstones Discussion Project

The Touchstones Discussion Project is a nonprofit organization founded on the belief that all people can benefit from the listening, speaking, thinking, and interpersonal skills gained by engaging in active, focused discussions. Since 1984, Touchstones has helped millions of students and adults develop and improve these skills in school, work, and life. For more information about the Touchstones Discussion Project, visit www.touchstones.org.

© 2003, 2006
by Touchstones Discussion Project
522 Chesapeake Avenue
Annapolis, Maryland 21403
(800) 456-6542
www.touchstones.org

All rights reserved. No part of this book—except worksheets explicitly noted for classroom use—may be reproduced in any form without prior consent of the authors.

ISBN: 1-878461-71-0

Acknowledgments

We would like to thank the following for their help in the publication of this volume:

The National Gallery of Art, Washington D.C., for permission to reproduce B-1029 *Prisoners Listening to Music* by Käthe Kollwitz.

Harper's Bazaar for permission to reprint excerpts from *Almos' a Man* by Richard Wright. Copyright 1940.

Contents

Unit 2: Exploratory Writing

Unit 3: Teaching Oneself

Introduction

After one year of Touchstones Discussions, students have changed, at different rates, and in both simple and complex ways. When you think back on those first five or six classes using Touchstones Volume I and compare them with the last classes of the year, the differences are significant. Early classes were chaotic—sometimes five or six students spoke at once, side conversations continually occurred, and students expected you to take the lead. Students raised their hands, addressed their remarks to you, and everyone, probably including you, felt uncomfortable with periods of silence. In comparison, students exhibited much different behaviors in the last classes of the first year. They listened more thoughtfully, looked to the group for responses, and were comfortable with short periods of silence.

It is not surprising that these changes require a year of work and effort by you and your students. Changes like these are much less external and behavioral than they seem. Changing behaviors requires redefining and modifying the students' expectations and habits about what is appropriate in a classroom and changing students' attitudes toward a school activity. Last year, many students recognized that their roles as students could be changed. Further, the students realized that they could take ownership of their education and that this appropriation involved both opportunities and responsibilities. These realizations were the principle goals of the first year.

More complex changes—active listening, asking relevant questions, and genuine cooperation with others—require even greater effort. Last year's changes in behavior made a start toward these changes. In the second year of Touchstones, using Touchstones Volume II, students begin to modify their roles as individuals, learn to cease being only students, and to take on the role of teacher. Helping students learn to teach themselves is the principle goal of this second year of Touchstones Discussions.

The Goal of Touchstones Volume II

As teachers, one of our purposes, if not our ultimate purpose, is to enable our students to free themselves from dependence on us. Although on occasion we acknowledge that people do in fact teach themselves, it rarely happens as a result of an explicit set of skills. Rather, it occurs in an occasional and often accidental way. When people have learned something they did not previously know, and we cannot identify a teacher (either a person who is an expert, a self-teaching manual, a textbook, or a software program), we conclude that those people have taught themselves. Yet we are uncomfortable with this conclusion because it appears paradoxical. We are claiming that a person is both student and teacher; that he or she is simultaneously the one who does not know and the person who knows. Such a claim cuts to the heart of the concepts and structures, the expectations and behaviors that organize the technological world within which we live. Developing the skill of teaching oneself requires adjusting concepts and behaviors as well as exploring and practicing new notions of teaching and learning. The Touchstones format is specifically constructed in order to allow this experimentation and practice.

Changing the Roles of Students

All of our students have developed their own pictures of themselves as students. They believe they are interested or disinterested in school, or that they are talented or weak in various subjects. Two factors that contribute to these pictures are the disconnect between the time students spend in school and the time they spend out of school, and the stories students develop about their own abilities and limitations.

Many, if not most, students view their lives as partitioned into two unconnected spheres of activity—time in school and time outside of school. The time students spend outside of school constitutes their "real lives." Time spent in school is often viewed as unrelated to students' real lives, and therefore carries less personal meaning than time spent out of school. This disconnect is one of the root causes of disengagement among students. In order for engagement in one school activity to transfer to other school and non-school activities, students must re-think their attitudes toward themselves and school and explore the beliefs and feelings that lead them to see school work as external and tangential to their real concerns.

The partition that students feel between their personal and school life is not an unfamiliar one in modern society. Adults often share this sense of division between their private and work lives. Many adults feel a lack of interpenetration and reinforcement between work life and private life, and often believe the two to be characteristically opposed to one another. In the professional or public realm, objectivity, strict organizational structures, and a critical stance are considered vital; while subjectivity, spontaneity, closeness, and trust characterize the personal realm.

The school, no less than the corporation or other social structure, is an institution within public society. Its organizational procedures display a set of priorities seemingly in opposition to students' personal lives—objectivity vs. subjectivity, strict organization vs. spontaneity, and skepticism vs. trust are a few examples. The separation and opposition between our personal and professional lives creates a tension between the two that may allow one realm to inappropriately dominate the other. The question for teachers is how not only to engage students in class or generally in school, but how to help students find a connection between their personal lives and their school lives.

Touchstones Volume I marks out an academic format in which the students' concerns, opinions, and experiences have a legitimate place. Last year, you may have seen some students become engaged in the discussions despite their efforts to remain apathetic. However, interest in one class does not imply that students will become interested in school or recognize that school has more than an abstract connection to their lives. In Touchstones Volume II, the priorities of school and life are brought to the surface, discussed, and reflected on. When brought to the surface, the connection and mutually complementary aspects of the public and personal can be explored.

Students not only often feel disengaged from school but, even when motivated, can be blocked from participation because of self-developed stories about which subjects interest them and what skills they possess. From very early on in their educational experience, students judge their own abilities and limitations, particularly in mathematics, science, and writing. Their often-erroneous judgments lead students to develop stories about themselves—that they either are or are not math people, science people, or writers.

There may be many reasons for these stories—low test scores on aptitude tests, hostility or uneasiness toward certain subjects, past failures in particular subjects, or peer pressure to avoid learning certain skills. Whatever the reasons for them, the stories are a decisive factor in determining what students feel is possible for them, and they are manifested in actual student achievement. Students view themselves as being good or bad at math or writing. These views lead to results that reinforce students' stories—they become academic self-fulfilling prophecies. Students who believe they are incapable perform poorly, and their poor performance reinforces their perception of their abilities. And, many times, students who believe they are good at school perform well but without depth or examination. These "good" students often feel that they are playing a game with teachers—trading correct answers and good behavior for good grades or other rewards. And here as well, rewards and good grades reinforce the idea that students are doing well and that nothing more is expected of them. Changing this pernicious cycle requires that students break through these roles and fears by recognizing their true strengths and weaknesses and learning to improve upon them. Part of the goal of the second year is to help students realize the connections between their two roles—student and non-student—and to encourage them to examine, and reconstruct if necessary, their roles in school. These goals are necessary steps for students to learn to teach themselves.

The Three Units in this Volume

Unit I: Cooperating Through Differences—Student as Leader & Participant

In order to teach themselves, students must clearly discern their own limitations, learn how to move beyond these limitations through the strengths and skills of others, and learn from others where none possess expertise. The first stage of learning to teach oneself, therefore, involves a heightened form of cooperation in which students teach and learn from one another. In Unit I of this Guide, the students progress from cooperating in spite of their differences to cooperating through their differences.

In Touchstones Volume I, cooperation required establishing a level at which the similarities among students could manifest themselves. Despite differences in reading, speaking, and writing skills; differences in the need for certainty and clarity; and differences in the ability to express one's opinion or give evidence for one's opinion, students learn to cooperate through a similarity that unites them. This similarity is an unfamiliarity with the discussion process. The formats of the discussion and the texts are equally alien to the students and force them to establish a common ground on which to work together. Cooperation through similarities requires a distinction between leader, or expert, and participant, or non-expert.

In Touchstones Volume II, the recognition and acknowledgement that every member of the group has a different set of strengths and weaknesses, and that each member's set is valuable, is crucial. It is what allows students to utilize one another's strengths, and help one another improve on weaknesses—essentially, to cooperate better because they are different, not in spite of their differences. Cooperation that utilizes group members' similarities rather than their differences is valuable, however for students to teach themselves, they must not gloss over their differences, but examine them, make them explicit, and learn to utilize their own and others' strengths. Unit I begins this process by encouraging students to think as both leader and participant. Where there is no leading expert, each member of the group learns to simultaneously adopt the two perspectives of the participant and leader. This dual perspective encourages students to think about how to utilize one another's skills in improving the discussions, and prepares them to think about how to utilize others' skills and knowledge when attempting to teach themselves.

Unit II: Exploratory Writing—Student as Writer and Reader

The bridge from learning with others without expertise to teaching oneself is accomplished through exploratory writing. Students engage in this form of writing throughout the second year, principally in Unit II.

Writing, in the context of Touchstones, is distinct from essay or report writing in other classes. There, the model is often that a student gathers material through research, reading, or experience and develops ideas that he or she learns to express and make public for others through writing. The student first possesses something—an idea, a thought—and then makes it external for others in writing. In Touchstones, students' writing does not assume a pre-existent idea. Rather, writing is an activity in which ideas and thoughts emerge and an arena for exploration and thinking. Though the writing is sometimes shared, its primary purpose is to be the process by which the writer recognizes and takes possession of his or her own idea or thought. The writer is, therefore, also the principal reader. In this form of writing, the students write about themselves; they will teach themselves. This structure sets the stage for Unit III, in which the students teach themselves more explicitly.

Unit III: Teaching Oneself—Student as Teacher and Student

The third unit focuses on enabling students to explore and practice how to teach themselves. To achieve this, they must recognize clearly what they do and do not know. They must be able to discern whether what they do not know and need to learn is the kind of subject matter that one can teach oneself. In cases where one cannot teach oneself the subject matter, such as a formula in physics or in mathematics, a part of teaching oneself is deciding who can teach what one needs to learn. In addition, once the knowledge is learned, one must be able to apply and extrapolate the models and problems of that learning experience to new and real situations. All forms of extrapolation involve teaching oneself. Students learn to move into uncharted terrain without becoming paralyzed by the uncertainty that characterizes such exploration. Practice in these specific skills occurs in Unit III of this Guide.

The Transition from *Touchstones Volume I* to *Touchstones Volume II*

Beginning the Second Year

In Touchstones Volume II students undertake the task of teaching themselves, which means learning together what they collectively do not know. To achieve this, they have to learn how to think responsibly about new ideas and situations, learn how to guide their own inquiry, and how to ask others for assistance. The development of these skills is encouraged by the texts, which are from a widely diverse authorship, and by a new supplemental activity—writing.

Although your students have had experience with Touchstones Volume I, it will be unusual for them to have previously worked together. You should, therefore, not be surprised by problems of group formation and dominance in the group. Your students are aware of the nature of those problems and how they should deal with them. However, applying what they know to a new situation and a new group of individuals requires effort. The progress is accelerated by beginning this year with variations on two exercises from the Touchstones Volume I, which should be done in the first two classes. One of these involves the ground rules; the other asks students to complete and then discuss a questionnaire about student attitudes toward discussion. In the first class, a text from Volume I is used. However, this text is used in a new way that is appropriate to the change in goals for Volume II.

Class Structure

The class meets once a week for one forty-five minute period. The texts are roughly the same length as in Volume I, as is the language level. There are both small group exercises and large group discussions; however, now that the students have at least one year of experience, the large group discussions dominate.

Largely, the difference between Touchstones Volumes I and II is one of degree—Volume II extends and expands on the work of Volume I. One of the main differences involves opening questions. Students using Volume I write down opening questions but students' questions generally are not used to open discussion. In Volume II, each student is given time to write down a question, and a process of random selection is used to select the opening question from among these. Some questions will be clear, brief, and apt, others will not. However, even when the opening question is confusing, it is not your job to reformulate or alter the question. The entire class undertakes this task with your assistance.

The Texts

Over the course of Volume I, the texts became more prominent in the discussion. At first, it was used to initiate discussion and to develop certain skills. Midway through the second stage of Volume I, and increasingly in the third unit on listening, did the text share equal status with the students' experiences and the group process. Yet the text never became the central focus of the discussion. Rather, it became a touchstone, a tool by means of which the students as individuals and as a group made their own opinions explicit and engaged in group exercises.

In Touchstones Volume II, the text's role becomes more pronounced. To achieve the goal of the second year, the skill of teaching oneself, students need to clarify, discuss, and, when appropriate, modify two sets of attitudes each of us possesses. One set of attitudes characterizes how we are expected to behave and perform in the institutional framework of a technology-driven society. The other set of attitudes characterize our personal lives and relations with friends and relatives. Each text explicitly addresses aspects of one of these sets of attitudes, or portrays an unexpected mixture of the two. In this way, the texts play an essential role in the discussion while always remaining a tool, rather than the focus.

The Discussion

The very process and form of Touchstones Discussions also enter the picture as a crucial component. The discussion is both similar to and quite different from the format of a regular class and the discussions that occur with friends and family. As such, the discussion format blends these seemingly opposed sets of attitudes and can help illuminate both the texts and participants opinions. The relationships among these three components—the texts, the class structure, and our attitudes—become more pervasive than in Volume I, and are more explicitly addressed.

Texts, Technological Attitudes, & Teaching Oneself

For over a century, people in modern society have drawn up lists of "classic" books— works considered to be especially important either because they were thought to have played an important part in the emergence of the technological world or because they expressed well the concerns of people who live in such a world. List making organizes and establishes an order of importance among things—a common activity in a society that is increasingly based on scientific processes and thinking. But producing a list also requires the elimination of items that do not fit the list-maker's criteria. The exclusion of "less important" elements is often necessary. There is so much information currently available that we would be lost if we did not rely on someone's determination of what is important. However, it is crucial that we do not simply continue to organize, order, and exclude as a matter of habit. We must determine when such an approach is helpful and when it is harmful—ultimately, a determination that each of us must make for ourselves.

Many thinkers have recognized that certain forms of exclusion are harmful. Many works of authors living in non-technological societies, or of those who living in a technological society but not at its center, have been found to rival traditional classics in quality, depth, and seriousness. They differ from the classics in their literary style, approach, and attitudes toward society and community. In Touchstones Volume II, these two kinds of texts—the classics and the previously excluded works—play different but complementary roles in reaching the goal of this project.

As discussed earlier, students with all levels of interest in school experience a lack of continuity between their school and personal lives, a lack of continuity that adults also express. All of us, as individuals, and as members of society, have pushed the set of attitudes that characterizes our personal lives to one side to make room for those prized by our society.

Since our earliest years, we have been acquiring attitudes that have helped us get along in the technological world. Among the beliefs that have shaped us are the following:

1. Objectivity is an important quality;
2. A critical and skeptical manner is necessary;
3. Efficiency is praiseworthy;
4. Problems should have definite solutions;
5. Correct solutions come from professionals;
6. Organization is essential;
7. Situations should always be controlled; and
8. Risk-taking should be minimized.

The eight statements above form the basis of modern science and technology. As science and technology have increasingly created the shape of our world, the above beliefs have increasingly shaped our lives. And with good reason! Without them we could not survive in the technological world. Yet we have also acquired attitudes that have helped us to prosper in our personal lives. The following list characterize these attitudes:

1. Subjectivity and subjective responses are of paramount importance;
2. Trust is the foundation of relationships among people;
3. Spontaneity is praiseworthy;
4. Problems are solved through compromises;
5. Compromises must come from the people most directly involved;
6. Long-range goals determine how or whether one organizes one's time;
7. Openness to new situations; and
8. Risk-taking is necessary.

These core attitudes of our personal lives are often sidelined for the increasing prominence of the science and technology in our world.

While all of these attitudes are familiar to us, they often go unrevealed. The classic and non-classic texts in Volume II exemplify, articulate, or attempt to justify one or more of these attitudes, thus acting as a mirror in which students can see the operation of the attitudes in themselves, perhaps for the first time. The readings were selected with the aim of understanding the two sets of attitudes, to be better able to use them when appropriate, and to modify them if they are not appropriate.

The texts are also a tool that students can use to discuss the differences between themselves and others without expressing that difference in a critical or antagonistic way. Students discover in discussion that some people are public creatures, others are scrupulously private; some incessantly desire objectivity, others subjectivity; some seek experts to solve their problems, others figure things out on their own; some are always suspicious and critical, others are trusting or even gullible; some hold fast to evidence and seek more before acting, others risk acting upon little to no evidence at all. Working on a common task with the presence of such differences, each student develops the skill of cooperating with people whose outlooks, backgrounds, and abilities are different from his or her own. In this way, Volume II encourages cooperation by means of differences, rather than cooperation in spite of differences.

The nature of the discussion format requires participants to recognize the ways in which we must each blend the two sets of attitudes explored above. For instance, the desire for objectivity must be tempered, since genuine participation in discussion utilizes participants' experiences, feelings, and beliefs. Yet subjective and personal responses to a text need to be presented in a responsible manner, so that others can share, build on, and criticize them. Similarly, skepticism and critical postures must also be modified by openness and trust among group members, and the desire to cover material efficiently must be subordinated to the long-range goals of improving group process. In the first year, the class as a whole learned blend the attitudes described above in order to teach itself. Now, in the second year, all students, by personally melding the technological and personal attitudes manifested in Touchstones Discussions, learn to teach themselves.

Learning to teach oneself is not just a fine idea. In today's world, it is a necessary skill. Within our rapidly changing institutions, people must be able to think and act responsibly in situations where there are neither models nor precedents. New dimensions in problem solving abilities are required. In addition, our students, whatever their future role in society, must learn how to think cooperatively and work as a member of a team composed of individuals with diverse backgrounds, skills, and abilities. In order to think cooperatively (which does not mean adopting the opinions of the most powerful or articulate members of the group), students must learn how to take intellectual risks. This requires courage to explore ideas publicly and to accept correction from others without experiencing a sense of failure or inadequacy. In short, the students need to be able to learn from others who are neither experts nor professionals, and then to take the next step to learn to teach themselves. Uncertainty must be viewed as a source of possibility and change, as well as an invitation to re-examine our opinions. In other words, uncertainty must not lead to paralysis but to action—the action of teaching oneself.

How to Use this Guide

This teacher's guide contains thirty lesson plans divided into three units of ten lessons each. Each lesson plan contains an introductory section that orients you to the issue or skill that concerns the class in that meeting. These introductory sections indicate the connection of one lesson plan with the previous ones, highlight concepts that appear in the text for that meeting, discuss the skills that are being developed, or suggest general lines of approach that you might explore in the discussion. Following this introduction, there is a short summary of the lesson that focuses on specific links between the individual and small group work and the culminating large group discussion. There is also a list of possible questions to raise during the discussion, even though most of your discussions will be opened by students' questions. Do not feel that you should address any or all of these questions. Their use is entirely optional. The segments of the lesson are laid out on a timeline in the lesson plan. The lesson plan is a suggested timeframe—you should feel free to modify the class as you see fit.

On the worksheet, you will find students' individual and small group activities. The lessons vary quite a bit in these preparatory activities, and again, you should feel free to add, delete, or modify these activities to suit your class's needs. The worksheets, which appear in each lesson and ask the student to respond to particular questions, must be duplicated and distributed to the students. Sometimes the worksheets are completed in class. Generally they are out-of-class assignments to be completed before the students come to class. When preparation is required of students, it is important that all students prepare. Building the expectation among students that they will all prepare the assignment is an important element of building trust within the group. Each student should have a notebook in which to keep the worksheets and writing assignments.

The bulk of class time is devoted to small group work and large group discussion. The small group work concentrates on investigating the various perspectives presented in students' individual work. Sometimes, the small group will attempt to come to consensus, and sometimes the small group must make a joint decision on a specific issue. In all cases, individual and small group work initiate and focus the students' attention on various issues, behaviors and concepts brought up by the text. The preliminary work is preparation for the large group discussion.

The Volume II Teacher's Guide is a set of signposts, suggestions, and general structures. Your class is not a class in general but one with very individual members that will develop a history entirely its own. The concepts and skills that are introduced are not intended to be entirely understood or mastered before moving to the next lesson. They will reappear in various guises throughout the year. Touchstones adapts a long-range perspective on students' progress. The year is cumulative in terms of experiences, not cumulative with respect to content, as is the case in traditional classes.

Recollecting the Previous Year

You are probably working with a new Touchstones group this year. Although, as individuals, your students have become skilled in discussion through their experience using Touchstones Volume I, they need to revive these skills and apply them in a new situation. Your students are like a brand new group in one crucial respect: many of them are not aware that they possess discussion skills. Many of them will assume that the progress they made during the first year depended on a particular teacher or a particular group of students who somehow got along together. The students will not clearly remember the difficulties they faced in the first six to eight discussion sessions, and therefore will not recognize their improvements or their increased skill. One of the goals of Touchstones Volume II is for students to become aware of the skills they possess and learn how to build on these to acquire the skills they lack. Another goal is to help students make their implicit assumptions, attitudes, and basic beliefs explicit, and to consciously modify and elaborate on them, if necessary.

Worksheet 1 prepares students for the coming work in two ways. First, it models the kind of work that will be pursued throughout the year—students are asked to consider themselves both as individuals and as members of a group. Second, the questions lead the students to reflect on their skills, weaknesses, and attitudes toward a common experience—the Touchstones class. This activity will bring up some of the underlying assumptions on which students will focus over the course of the year.

To begin the second year, it is useful to hold a discussion on an early text from *Touchstones Volume I*. The text we will use is *About Revenge*, by Sir Francis Bacon. Many students nostalgically remember that first discussion concerning revenge. However, they are, in general, inaccurately remembering the class. It is doubtful that their first discussion on revenge was a true discussion at all. The students probably argued with one another about whether it was right to get even. A few students probably dominated, and some students shared personal experiences that were not very relevant. In other words, the students did not have the skills to deal with the dynamics that arose during their early discussions. By arguing, feeling frustrated, and bringing up personal experiences, the students began to recognize, what they needed to do in order to tame those dynamics and work together. By taking responsibility for that level of investment, students began to realize that they could feel ownership of a school activity, and that they could become invested in the activity at a level they considered important. Now, when beginning Touchstones Volume II, it is appropriate to hold another class on the same text, and to give the students the opportunity to compare that first discussion with this one. On reviewing their memories, they will begin to recognize that they have changed and developed skills. Articulating the differences between that first discussion and this one will set the stage for examining their own growth and development.

Lesson Plan 1

1. TEXT AND QUESTIONS..5 minutes
   - Give the students time to complete the first two questions.

2. RESPONSES..6 minutes
   - Invite three or four volunteers to present their responses.
   - Ask students whether anyone answered the two questions differently.
   - *Note:* It is likely that students' reasons will provide insight into their attitudes. For instance, a student might say that a) it is hard not to get involved in side conversations because people want to say what comes into their minds without waiting for their turn, or b) some people don't speak clearly because they don't want to be heard. Reason (a) indicates that spontaneity should be respected, while reason (b) points out the conflict between the desire to express an opinion and the fear of being wrong. This conflict often leads students to speak, but inaudibly. Other answers don't bring up such attitudes, as in c) it is hard to speak to be heard because my voice is not strong enough. If student volunteers offer answers like (a) or (b), you should invite the group to discuss them.

3. TEXT..2 minutes
   - Read the text aloud as students follow along.

4. DISCUSSION..15 minutes
   - Open the discussion by reading the following passage from the text, "What is certain about planning to get even is that one's own wounds remain open. If one didn't spend one's time trying to take revenge, those injuries would heal and be forgotten." Ask the students whether they agree or disagree with the writer.
   - *Note:* In general this year, students' questions will initiate discussion. You should inform the students that they will take on this duty, but that in this first session you will ask the opening question.

5. DISCUSSION ANALYSIS..7 minutes
   - Ask the students how this discussion differs from the discussion they had last year on the same text.
   - Ask the students to think about any additional ground rules they would propose for this discussion group.
   - Remind students to obtain a three-ring binder or notebook to keep track of all of their worksheets and notes from their discussions.

Total: 45 minutes

Worksheet 1

Ground Rules

1. **Read the text carefully.** In Touchstones Discussions your opinions are important, but these opinions are your thoughts about the text.

2. **Listen to what others say and don't interrupt.** A discussion cannot occur if you don't listen carefully to what people say.

3. **Speak clearly.** For others to respond to your opinions, everyone must be able to hear and understand what you say.

4. **Give others your respect.** A discussion is a cooperative exchange of ideas and not an argument or a debate. Don't talk privately to your neighbor. You may become excited and wish to share your ideas, but in Touchstones this is done publicly for the whole class.

Individual Work

1. a) Which ground rule was hardest for you to follow last year?

   b) Why was this rule hard for you to follow?

2. a) Which ground rule was hardest for the class as a whole to follow last year?

   b) Why was this rule hard for your class to follow?

About Revenge
Francis Bacon

Revenge is a sort of savage justice. The more people try to take revenge, the more the law should punish them. When a man commits a crime, he breaks the law. But when the injured person takes revenge, the person destroys law itself. In taking revenge, a person does indeed get even with his enemy. But when one refuses to take revenge, he shows that he is better than his enemy. King Solomon, I am sure, said it is glorious for a person to forget an injury.

Whatever is past is gone and can't be changed. Wise people know they have enough to do in the present and with whatever might happen in the future. They don't spend their time taking revenge. People who spend their time worrying about past injuries just waste their time. Also, no person hurts another person just to hurt him. Rather, it is done for his profit or his own pleasure or his honor or for some other reason he might have. So why should I be angry with someone for loving himself better than he loves me? Suppose someone hurts me because he is evil. Isn't that just like a thorn or briar that scratches me because it can't do anything else?

Revenge is most allowable when there is no specific law to correct an injury. However, one must then be careful that the kind of revenge one takes does not break yet another law.

Some people when they get even want their enemy to know that it will happen. This is a more generous way of acting. Not letting your enemy know you are going to get even is a cowardly thing to do. It is like killing at night from ambush.

There was an Italian ruler, Cosimo de Medici, who said the following to his friends who might betray or injure him: "We read," he said, "that we are commanded to forgive our enemies. But we never read that we are commanded to forgive our friends." I think, however, that the spirit of what Job said is truer. He said, "Shall we receive good from God and not also be willing to accept the evil." The same is true, in part, about friends.

What is certain about planning to get even is that one's own wounds remain open. If one didn't spend one's time trying to take revenge, those injuries would heal and be forgotten. Public or state revenges are, for the most part, good—as in the case of the murderers of Julius Caesar. Private revenges are, however, not good. People who take revenge live the life of witches. They cause trouble to others and come to a bad end.

Possible Questions to Raise

- Do you agree that if you spend your time planning revenge your own wounds will remain open?
- When is it okay to take revenge?
- How do you feel when you get revenge?
- What is the difference between public and private revenge?
- How was this discussion different from your discussion on the same text last year?
- Would you propose any additional ground rules for the group?

Motivation and Action

Toward the end of the first year, the students began to take control of their Touchstones Discussions. They chose a Touchstones text, prepared a reading, and made decisions about the structure of the class—whether there should be small group work and if so, what kind, and how long the large group discussion would last. In addition, they learned what problems a discussion leader faces, and had to make decisions about when to intervene as they conducted the classes. In the second year, although they will not select the readings, and you will determine the activities, their control of the situation will move to a new level. Over the course of the year, the students will learn how to be simultaneously discussion leaders and participants.

As the students gradually gain skills as individuals and as a group, your role will change too. However, you are never a passive observer of the situation. You remain the teacher. Sometimes you will act as you do in regular classes, by directing activities, giving writing assignments, and on occasion, disciplining students. At other times, you will act as a guide or an adviser. Sometimes you will be a participant. Yet even as a participant you will be the leader in the sense that you will be modeling what the students are trying to achieve.

This dual role may sound paradoxical. What appears to be most important to a participant is to express his or her individual perspective and opinion. Conversely, the role of the discussion leader appears to be entirely concerned with impartiality, and addressing the needs of the group. The discussion leader judges whether the group has stayed too close or moved too far from the text; whether the group is having problems with the ground rules; or whether certain participants are dominating the discussion. Participation and leadership therefore appear to involve different priorities and to be distinct, or even opposing, roles. You and your students are striving to achieve a balance between these two roles, so that none of you remains entirely personal (as participant) or entirely objective (as discussion leader).

What will become centrally important this year is to have students discern the underlying assumptions and attitudes that shape their opinions and responses. For example, some of us find it easier to criticize than to accept criticism; some of us can change our minds and opinions in public situations, while for many people it is difficult. These behaviors indicate basic assumptions on the part of the individual. For instance, the person who is unable to change his mind in public may believe on a basic level that changing one's mind is a sign of weakness. By interacting with others, these behaviors are revealed to us. We may see very different, or very similar, behaviors in others, or others may point out certain behaviors directly. We need one another to recognize our own behaviors. In our daily lives, we function in accordance with a set of basic assumptions. These assumptions define the way we see the world, and shape the way we understand and learn. Only in the process of serious, focused collaboration with other people can we begin to recognize that not all people operate on the same set of assumptions. As the students build awareness of one another, they begin to understand what other members of the group need, and the differences between the role of participant and the role of discussion leader diminish.

The worksheet asks the students to examine their attitudes toward Touchstones. They are asked to choose the reason that best explains a certain behavior. Students must think about the underlying causes of their own and others' attitudes and behaviors in the discussion.

The text for today's discussion is from Benjamin Franklin's *Autobiography.* In it, Franklin describes his attempt to improve himself in ways he knows he should. He observes his faults, and makes resolutions to improve. However, in spite of his resolve, his old habits and desires get in the way. He attempts to deal with this by methodically approaching the problem, and makes a notebook to keep track of his progress.

All of us have experienced roughly what Franklin recounts. We make resolutions and then break them, in spite of our good intentions. However, very few of us have tried Franklin's method. At the end of Lesson 2, students will make a resolution and begin keeping track of their successes and failures on a chart.

Lesson Plan 2

1. INDIVIDUAL WORK..15 minutes
    - Distribute copies of Worksheet 2.
    - Read the worksheet aloud and have students respond. When students finish this assignment, the worksheets should be put in their notebooks or binders.

2. TEXT...2 minutes
    - Read the text aloud and have students read along silently.

3. QUESTIONS..2 minutes
    - Have students form opening questions.
    - Ask for a volunteer to pose the opening question.

4. DISCUSSION...18 minutes
    - If the opening question receives no response from the class, ask the students if they can reformulate it. Give the students a great deal of latitude in the first ten minutes of the discussion.

5. RESOLUTION CHART...8 minutes
    - Distribute copies of the Resolution Chart to the students.
    - Ask the students to think about how they as individuals would like to improve as participants in Touchstones Discussions, and have them write it as a resolution on the Resolution Chart. Their resolution must concern the way they wish to improve in discussions.
    - Tell the students that they will be keeping a record on each of the next five classes concerning their progress.
    - Have the students write a few sentences on how they tried to keep their resolution in this discussion, whether they think they succeeded, or if not, what caused their lack of success.
    - Ask the students to think about the last two discussions over the next week and to suggest a new or modified ground rule for the group.
    - Tell them that in Lesson 8 they will look at the success or lack of success in sticking to their resolutions.

Total: 45 minutes

Worksheet 2

Individual Work

You may recognize some of the behaviors described below. For each type of behavior, circle the reason that most likely explains why a person would behave that way. If you don't like any of the reasons provided, write your own answer for choice (d).

1. Marcia rarely speaks during the large group discussion, but she speaks in small groups and to friends outside of class.
   a) Marcia is afraid of being wrong in public.
   b) Marcia does not trust the group to take her opinions seriously.
   c) Marcia is shy, and will come out of her shell eventually.
   d) _____

2. Jermaine participates in discussions about mathematics and science but rarely about other works.
   a) Jermaine is not comfortable talking about his experiences.
   b) Jermaine needs to be certain about an answer before speaking.
   c) Jermaine likes these subjects and doesn't like others.
   d)_____

3. Sally only participates when she is correcting other people.
   a) Sally is most comfortable with a critical attitude.
   b) Sally wants to control the discussion.
   c) Sally does not believe other people want to hear her opinions.
   d)_____

4. Juan gets really good grades in other classes, but he hardly ever participates in Touchstones Discussions.
   a) Juan is bored in the discussions.
   b) Juan does not believe he can learn anything from other students.
   c) Juan doesn't think he can teach other students anything.
   d)_____

5. How do you participate in discussions? Briefly describe your participation, and give two or three reasons why you participate in that way.

Resolution Chart

Write a resolution concerning how you would like to improve your participation in the discussions. Keep this chart in your notebook, and track your progress over the next five discussions.

Resolution: _____

	I Improved	I didn't improve
Lesson 3 Why?	❏	❏
Lesson 4 Why?	❏	❏
Lesson 5 Why?	❏	❏
Lesson 6 Why?	❏	❏
Lesson 7 Why?	❏	❏

The Autobiography
Benjamin Franklin

Early in my life, I conceived the bold and difficult project of arriving at moral perfection. I wished to live without committing any fault at any time. I wanted to conquer all the faults that my desires, the customs of my society, and the urging of my friends might lead me into. Since I knew, or thought I knew, what was right and wrong, I did not see why I might not always do the one and avoid the other. But I soon found that I had undertaken a task of more difficulty than I had imagined.

While my attention was taken up in guarding against one fault, I was often surprised by another. This is because I was in the habit of committing this fault, and my habit took advantage of my inattention to it. Also, my desires were too strong for my reason. I finally realized that although my mind was convinced that it was in my interest to act rightly, that belief was not enough to prevent me from slipping and continuing to commit faults. I had to break my old bad habits, and acquire new good ones before I could depend on myself to act morally in a steady way. For this purpose, I invented the following method.

I made a list of the moral virtues I wanted to acquire. There were thirteen of them. To give an example of my method, I will talk about the one I call "order." By "order," I meant that I should arrange all aspects of my life so that I would always have enough time to do what I needed to do. My plan was to train myself to be in the habit of acting according to these virtues. I decided, therefore, not to practice them all together, but to practice them one at a time, and not to move on to the next until I had mastered the previous one.

To do this, I made a little notebook in which I devoted a page to each of the virtues. Every day, I made a note in the notebook whenever I failed to fulfill a particular one. I decided to give a week to practicing each virtue. Since there were thirteen of them, I had made up a thirteen week course in moral virtue. I followed this plan for quite a long time. In the end, I found that I had made some progress in self-management, except that I couldn't correct my faults with respect to order. Now that I am old, and my memory is bad, this fault bothers me even more.

I didn't arrive at the perfection I had aimed at but fell far short of it. However, I became a better and happier man by the effort than I would have been if I hadn't tried at all. Thus, I was like a person who wanted to have the beautiful handwriting of experts. Even if his writing never gets as good as the expert's, it does get better than it might have been otherwise.

Possible Questions to Raise

- What successes or failures have you had with keeping resolutions?
- Is Franklin's method a good one?
- Can you think of a method for keeping a resolution that might work better than Franklin's?

How Should We Govern Ourselves?

In the first class of the year, the students reviewed and discussed the ground rules. They also considered whether other ground rules might be useful. Most groups need the ground rules to be addressed explicitly in the beginning. The group did not pick out its own ground rules—their teacher and this *Guide* imposed the rules on the students. Therefore, so far the Touchstones ground rules are justified solely by the power of an external authority.

In many cases, the students' reactions to the ground rules are dictated by their attitudes toward the imposition of authority rather than by the content of the rules. Some students follow rules because they want to please the teacher; others break the rules precisely because they have an impulse to resist authority. As the students moved through Touchstones Volume I, they began to adhere to the ground rules, not because they were imposed on them, but because the students began to see the usefulness of the rules. The transition from being ruled by an external authority to self-governance is extended in Lesson 3.

In Lesson 2, the students made resolutions about how they could improve as individual discussion participants. In Lesson 3, you and your students will make a resolution for the entire group by choosing a new or modified ground rule for your Touchstones Discussions. Students may add to, modify, or keep intact the original four ground rules, and in this case, all decisions will be made by majority rule. The problem that the students must address is how group decision-making should occur. Each student should come to class with a suggestion for a new ground rule that will help the class improve. The group will need to discuss these various perspectives, diagnose the problem, and propose a solution. They will work in small groups and in the large group discussion to arrive at an objective diagnosis and a proposal for a new ground rule. The rule they choose may be one of the rules their classmates suggest or an entirely new one. All possibilities can be explored through today's group work, the worksheet, and Douglass's text on majority rule.

Is Government by the Majority Right? by Frederick Douglass, provides an argument for governing by majority rule. In the activities for Lesson 3, your students experiment with majority rule on two levels to determine the new ground rules for their own activity. First, the groups must reach consensus or devise some other method to determine a pool of possible new ground rules. Second, the entire class explicitly exercises majority rule in its selection procedure. These activities will help illustrate the range of issues that come up when majority rule is exercised, and will provide them with a shared experience of the consequences of majority rule. One avenue that you may want to explore is what possible alternatives there are to majority rule.

Lesson Plan 3

1. INDIVIDUAL WORK..10 minutes
   - Distribute Worksheet 3 to the students.
   - Ask student volunteers to read the four rules aloud.
   - Ask the students to answer questions 1 only.

2. SMALL GROUP WORK...10 minutes
   - Break the class into three groups.
   - Have the groups suggest a new ground rule and give a reason for it.
   - Have each group report on its new rule and the reason for it, and list the suggested rules on the board.

3. VOTE...8 minutes
   - Have students vote on each rule in turn. Each rule for which the majority votes will become a new ground rule. You will have seven votes total: one each for the original four, plus the three new rules proposed by the groups.
   - Tell students that the new set of ground rules will be those chosen by the majority and will go into effect immediately with this discussion.

4. INDIVIDUAL WORK, PART 2...2 minutes
   - After the rules have been decided upon, ask them to complete questions 2 and 3 on the worksheet.

5. TEXT...2 minutes
   - Read the text aloud as students follow along silently.

6. DISCUSSION..12 minutes
   - Discuss the text for the first eight to ten minutes, and then address whether or not the students think they did a good job with the new ground rules.

7. RESOLUTION CHART...1 minute
   - Remind the students to fill out their Resolution Chart from Lesson 2 on whether they individually improved in the way they wanted to in the last class.

Total: 45 minutes

Worksheet 3

Individual Work

1. Write down a new ground rule that you would propose for the group. Why do you think that the new rule might be necessary?

Small Group Work

1. As a group, compare your new rules and then choose one that you all agree on.

Individual Work, Part 2

2. Write down the rule the class decided upon.

3. Below are listed five ways a new ground rule could be selected for the group. Rank them best to worst (1 is best, 5 is worst).

_____ An outside expert.

_____ One person within the group.

_____ A small group of "serious" students.

_____ A majority of the group.

_____ Decide only if everyone can agree.

Is Government by the Majority Right?
Frederick Douglass

Were we to make an inquiry into the rightfulness of government by the majority, we should begin by assuming, first, that man is a social as well as an individual being. He is endowed by his Creator with faculties and powers suited both to his individuality and society. Second, individual isolation is unnatural, unprogressive and against the highest interest of man. Society is required by the natural wants and necessities of human existence. Third, man is born with reason and understanding, capable of discriminating between good and evil, right and wrong, justice and injustice. Fourth, while man is constantly liable to do evil, he is still capable of understanding and pursuing that which is good. Upon the whole, his evil tendencies are quite outweighed by the powers within him moving him toward good. Fifth, rewards and punishments are natural agents for restraining evil and for encouraging good, because man is endowed with faculties keenly alive to both. Finally, whatever serves to increase the happiness; to preserve the well being; to give permanence, order, and attractiveness to society; and leads to the very highest development of human perfection is, unless positively prohibited by Divine command, to be considered innocent and right. The question is: Is majority government right? Note that the question is not: Is arbitrary, despotic, tyrannical, corrupt, unjust, capricious government right? Rather, the question is: Is a society (that is, a company of human beings) right when it is authorized by their Creator to institute a government for themselves where the majority rules, and to pass and enforce laws that are in accordance with justice, liberty, and humanity?

Why should we show this respect to the majority? The answer is, simply because a majority of human hearts and intellects may be presumed, as a general rule, to take a wiser and more comprehensive view of the matters upon which they act than the minority. It is in accordance with the doctrine that good is the rule, and evil the exception in the character and constitution of man. If the facts were otherwise, that is, if men were more disposed to evil than to good, then it would, indeed, be dangerous for men to enter into an agreement by which power should be wielded by the majority. For then, evil being predominant in man, it would predominate also in the mass of men, and innumerable hardships would be inflicted upon good people. The old assertion of the wickedness of the masses, and their consequent unfitness to govern themselves, is the falsehood and corruption out of which have sprung the tyrannical conspiracies, calling themselves governments, in the old world.

Possible Questions to Raise

- What do you think of Douglass's statement that, "A majority of human hearts and intellects may be presumed, as a general rule, to take a wiser and more comprehensive view of the matters upon which they act than the minority"?
- What alternatives are there to majority rule?
- How do we use majority rule in American society?
- Would you have preferred another method of group decision-making to voting in today's activity?
- How did today's exercise change or confirm your ideas about majority rule?
- How well did we adhere to the new set of ground rules in our discussion?

Evidence and Belief

The advances of technology and fast-paced innovation of modern life are largely due to the acceptance of scientific examination as the standard by which knowledge and action are to be judged. Such "soft" sciences as psychology and sociology are increasingly attempting to use the randomized experimentation models of the "harder" sciences—biology, physics, and chemistry. As teachers, you have seen an increased emphasis placed on scientific research and uniform educational standards and testing. These trends all mark the existence of an assumption, which may or may not be entirely credible—that the ultimate goal is to approach every exploration from an objective stance. The corollary assumption is that human motives, passions, goals, and needs are corrupting influences that may prevent humans from seeing things as they actually are. In Lesson 4, your students will confront a feeling that is related to this tension between the objective and the subjective—the attitude of suspicion, or in its more scientific form, skepticism.

The text for Lesson 4, *On Suspicion*, was written by Sir Francis Bacon almost four hundred years ago. In the text, Bacon addresses many of the ways a suspicious attitude can be dangerous, and how one might avoid the pitfalls of being suspicious. However, your students may not have thought about the causes and consequences of suspicion in great detail. One of the topics that must come up in a discussion on suspicion is the nature and necessity of evidence. When we think of suspicion on a personal level, it is often thought to be a negative attitude, characterized by a lack of trust for others. We must seek out evidence to either confirm or deny our suspicions. A scientist must continually view himself with suspicion, and root out any possible biases or emotions that may corrupt the objective integrity of his work. However, the skepticism with which a scientist views the world is usually considered positive—in fact, the work of a scientist can become less valuable if it is found that he has not taken the appropriate steps to ensure that his own biases and feelings have not affected the outcome of his work. He must produce evidence of his objectivity in order to convince his audience of the validity of his work.

Bacon's text looks at how a stance or attitude that is useful, or even essential, in certain parts of our lives can be destructive when it is taken too far. He looks at the cases in which we become suspicious of other people—friends, lovers, and family—and how suspicion can destroy those relationships. He then gives advice about how to deal with these kinds of thoughts. This text is helpful in bringing out dynamics that need to be overcome in order for cooperation to occur. The discussion of this text can take many fruitful routes. Possible topics include the similarities and differences between personal suspicion and objective skepticism, the necessity of evidence either to confirm or deny suspicions, the place of emotions and biases within the context of different types of investigation, and the importance of objectivity. You might also ask students what roles suspicions, objectivity, and evidence play within the context of their discussions.

Lesson Plan 4

1. Individual Work..10 minutes
   - Distribute a worksheet to each student and ask the students to answer questions 1 and 2.

2. PAIR WORK...10 minutes
   - Try to pair each student with someone they do not know very well.
   - Ask each pair to come up with suggestions for question 1.

3. TEXT...2 minutes
   - Read the text aloud as students follow along silently.

4. DISCUSSION..20 minutes
   - Ask for a volunteer to pose the opening question.
   - Note: The student may either ask about some part of the exercise, the text, or the general issue.
   - Whichever of these possible types of question is chosen, you should not attempt to modify the question or assist the class in responding to it. You should trust that eventually the students will take the direction that makes the most sense to them.
   - End the discussion by asking students to think of a method the class could use to randomly choose someone to ask the opening question in future discussions.

5. RESOLUTION CHART...3 minutes
   - Remind the students to fill out their Resolution Chart for Lesson 4.
   - Note: For Lesson 5, you will need to be prepared with a method of randomly picking a student to pose the opening question, such as picking a name out of a hat.

Total: 45 minutes

Worksheet 4

Individual Work

Think of a situation in which you became suspicious of someone—a relative, a friend, a class-mate, or someone you didn't know very well. Then answer the questions below.

1. Why did you become suspicious? (For example, did someone tell you bad things about that person, or did you see that person do something you didn't like, or something else?)

2. Were you right or wrong to have been suspicious? Why?

Pair Work

1. If you were suspicious or mistrustful of someone, what would you do? List three ways you might handle the situation.

    a)

    b)

    c)

2. Choose the best approach from above and explain why it is the best one.

On Suspicion
Sir Francis Bacon

Suspicions are to thoughts as bats are to birds. They always fly when the sun goes down. Suspicions should be repressed or at least kept in check, because they cloud the mind. They break up friendships and make it difficult to do business. Suspicions turn kings into tyrants, make husbands jealous, and make wise men sad and indecisive. They are defects of the brain, not of the heart, since they affect even brave men. Brave people are not hurt by their suspicions, because they have the courage to examine them to see if they are true or false. Cowardly people, however, are hurt by suspicions, because they believe them too quickly. There is nothing that makes a man more suspicious than his own ignorance. Therefore, people should cure themselves of suspicions by trying to learn more, and not by brooding over them.

What do you want out of people? Are the people we deal with everyday as good as saints? Isn't it true that people have their own interests, and will be more concerned about themselves than about other people? The best way to handle suspicions is to assume that they are true, but to deal with them as if they were false.

A man ought to use suspicions so that, if they are true, they will do him no harm. The suspicions that a person comes to on his own are harmless. They are like the buzzing of bees. Suspicions that have been put into a man's mind by the whisperings and stories of others are, like the stings of bees, harmful.

The best way for a person to find the road out of the forest of suspicions is to talk to the person he suspects. By this means, he will find out more of the truth than he knew before. He will also make the other person more careful not to give him further grounds for suspicion. But this should not be done with dishonest people. For, if they once know that they are suspected, they will never again tell the truth.

Possible Questions to Raise

- When is it good to be suspicious?
- When is it bad to be suspicious?
- What causes people to be suspicious of one another?
- How might skepticism and suspicion be similar attitudes? (You may need to provide examples of scientific skepticism. For instance, scientific results often are not accepted until an experiment has been repeated many times, in various locations, and under the supervision of different scientists.)
- How can we, as Bacon says we should, "assume that [suspicions] are true, but to deal with them as if they were false?"
- How much evidence should people give to support their opinions in a discussion?
- What is the difference between supporting something with evidence, and proving something with evidence?

Evidence, Risk, and Uncertainty

Functioning within an environment of uncertainty usually entails taking risks. Risk-takers are often admired in our society as possessing the qualities of adventurers who travel into the unknown. Yet many times, when it appears that someone has taken a risk, it turns out instead that the person was merely unaware of the possible consequences of the action or did not believe that any bad consequences would actually occur. This is not risk-taking in the true sense—it is more like making a mistake. Taking a risk involves knowing that one is taking a risk. It requires both knowledge and courage. Taking a risk requires evaluating possible consequences, and choosing an option that may result in loss or poor consequences. Many people don't take risks at all if they can help it. Some only take risks with close and trusted friends, where they are liable to be forgiven or comforted if it turns out badly. Few people can be considered true risk-takers, and these people have usually learned how to evaluate risk through experience. Evaluating risk is a skill that one learns. In today's class, the students will begin to explore what a risk is and when one should take a risk.

Touchstones Volume II is structured to help the students make their attitudes and roles explicit and decide that they can, when they wish, change those attitudes and roles. Changing behavior is frightening, and it requires taking risks. The students need to recognize the need for taking risks—both intellectually and socially—and that some risks are not worth taking. This latter difference involves discovering what goals are worth what risks. It involves understanding what a calculated risk is. Uncertainty is what makes risk-taking difficult. Much of modern life is devoted to eliminating uncertainty. We want to be able to predict the weather, social and economic changes, and the outcomes of most events or projects. When an irreducible element of uncertainty remains, people generally respond by seeking some sort of insurance, to protect them from negative consequences.

While caution is generally good, the avoidance of uncertainty also implies the avoidance of significant change. Every fundamental change involves some uncertainty. This, of course, is particularly paradoxical in a school environment, since our aim as teachers is to make significant changes possible for our students. Yet, clearly, some forms of risk and uncertainty are as destructive and dangerous as the avoidance of all risk. We then arrive at the notion of a calculated risk. A calculated risk allows us to deal with elements of uncertainty within a structure that applies some measure of control to the situation.

At the end of Lesson 4, you asked the students to propose a method for randomly selecting a member of the group to ask the opening question in the discussion. For Lesson 5, you should be prepared to pick a student randomly, either by pulling a name out of a hat or some other simple method. Picking a student randomly raises the level of risk for all participants, since the person selected will have no additional time to prepare the reading. The students may have to ask a question on a reading that doesn't interest them, or they may ask a question that other students are not interested in pursuing. The students may also worry that other members of the group will think that their question is stupid, or that other students will not understand what they are asking. By allowing students to devise and select the random method employed, you will provide them with a certain amount of control over the amount of risk they will have to take.

The Mortal Immortal, by Mary Shelley, is about a man who gradually discovers that he may have taken a great risk. The speaker has swallowed a drink made by his master, a philosopher. As the years pass, he begins to suspect that the drink may have caused him to live forever. People generally fear dying and imagine they want to live forever. Part of the fear of death is simply that it is unknown. Another part is that, since the risk of death is present at all times to all people, it exposes our vulnerability and uncertainty. The man in the story feels that he cannot endure the uncertainty of not knowing and yet also begins to feel he cannot endure the loneliness of immortality. This text gives the students the opportunity to explore when it is appropriate to take a risk and what, if anything, they should know in taking it. It also allows them to discuss why uncertainty is uncomfortable. However, this story also addresses the fact that in some cases, certainty may be worse.

Lesson Plan 5

1. INDIVIDUAL WORK..8 minutes
   - Ask the students to complete Worksheet 5.
   - Note: Some reasons the requirement of randomly selecting a student to open the discussion might be useful are that 1) it gives the students some practice in thinking quickly, 2) it makes everyone more responsible for the success of the class, 3) it helps students learn that other students will help them if their question is not suitable to begin a discussion, and 4) it helps everyone take a significant step toward becoming simultaneously leader and participant.
   - Ask for some volunteers to read their answers to question 2 aloud.

2. DISCUSSION, PART 1..10 minutes
   - Ask the group what might make people uneasy about this procedure of random selection.
   - Ask the students what the group can do to ease the situation, and help others feel comfortable.
   - Ask the students to suggest ways of choosing.
   - Note: Make sure that all the options are random and simple to create, such as picking students' names out of a hat, spinning a wheel with students' names on it, or putting each student's name on one card in a deck of playing cards and randomly picking a card.

3. VOTE...3 minutes
   - After some suggestions have been given, have the class vote on a method.
   - Note: It is important that the students choose the device of random selection. It gives them a sense of control, even though the purpose of their choice is essentially to make them more vulnerable.

4. TEXT...2 minutes
   - Read the text aloud as students read along silently.
   - Ask students to write down a question.

5. DISCUSSION, PART 2..10 minutes
   - Pick a student's name out of a hat (or use whatever method you have prepared) to decide who will start the discussion.
   - Note: Starting with Lesson 6, you will implement whatever randomizing procedure the students have voted to use. You may need to have a group of volunteers construct the device between this class and the next.
   - If the group does not respond to the question, ask for volunteers to rephrase the question.

6. WRITING ASSIGNMENT 5...10 minutes
   - After the discussion, ask the students to write one paragraph on how they would feel if they had taken the drink.

7. ASSIGNMENT...1 minutes
   - When they are finished, tell the students to rework the paragraph before the next class. Do not be too explicit in your instructions; merely tell them to work on it until they are satisfied with it.

8. RESOLUTION CHART..1 minute

Total: 45 minutes

Worksheet 5

Individual Work

1. What method should we use to randomly choose a student to ask the opening question?

2. Why might randomly choosing someone to ask the opening question be a useful way to start the discussion?

3. What would you say to encourage a student who was nervous about this change in the class?

Writing Assignment 5

1. Write a paragraph about how you would feel if you had taken the same drink as the man in the story. Keep the paragraph in your notebook.

The Mortal Immortal
Mary Shelley

When I slyly drank half of the strange drink that my master, the Philosopher Cornelius, made, I didn't know what it was. It was only at his death that I got a hint about it. He was sad that he hadn't drunk some himself before it spilled. He said it would have enabled him to live. I learned yet more about the drink when my wife of many years finally died. In our years together she had grown old and I had hardly changed at all. At her death, I felt I had lost all that had really bound me to humanity. Since then, how many cares have I had, and how few joys? I have been like a sailor without a rudder or a compass tossed on a stormy sea. Such have I been. In fact I have been more lost, more hopeless than such a sailor. A passing ship may save a lost sailor; but I have no beacon except the hope of death.

Death! Strange-faced friend of weak humanity! Why, alone of all mortals, have you kept me out of your sheltering fold? I return to my first question. Am I immortal? I drank only half the drink made by my master. Wasn't the whole of it necessary to complete the magic? So does that mean that I am only half immortal? But who can count half the years of eternity? I often try to imagine by what rule the infinite can be divided, and find no answer. Sometimes I fancy that old age is creeping up on me because I find one gray hair. Fool! Am I sad? Yes! Though I long for death, the fear of age and death still creeps coldly into my heart. The more I live, the more I dread death, even while I hate life. Man is a puzzle when he fights against the fixed laws of his nature, as I do.

I have often gazed on the blue depths of calm lakes, and the rushing of mighty rivers. I have felt that peace inhabits those waters. Yet, I have turned my steps away, to live yet another day. I have often asked myself whether suicide would be a crime for me since only by killing myself could the doors of the other world be opened to me. Thus have I lived on for many years, all alone and weary of myself, desiring death, yet never dying—a mortal immortal. Neither ambition nor greed enters my mind any longer. The strong love that eats at my heart, never to be returned—never to find an equal on which to spend itself—lives there only to torment me.

This very day I have conceived a plan by which I may end it all. I will depart on an expedition that no mortal body can possibly survive. Thus I shall finally put my immortality to the test and rest forever—or return, the wonder and benefactor of the human species. Before I go, a miserable pride has caused me to write these pages. I feel I mustn't die without leaving a name behind. Three hundred years have passed since I drank that magic drink. Another year shall not pass until I try to yield this body, this cage for my soul that thirsts for elements of fire and water. Or if, by chance, I survive and my name becomes famous among men, I shall choose even more desperate means. Somehow I shall scatter the atoms that make up me. I will free the life imprisoned within me, and so cruelly prevented from soaring from this dim earth to a place more suited to its immortal nature.

Possible Questions to Raise

- How risky is the journey planned by the character in The Mortal Immortal?
- Was drinking the potion a risk? Why or why not?
- Can you think of a time when you took a big risk?
- Can you think of a situation in which you wouldn't take any risks at all?

Competition

In previous lessons, students have examined a range of topics that address their individual behavior—both in life and in their discussion group. These topics have included private behavior and public behavior in Lesson 2; subjectivity and objectivity in Lesson 3; suspicion, evidence, and objectivity in Lesson 4; and risk and uncertainty in Lesson 5. Lesson 6 will again involve these concepts and attitudes in the process of examining another topic—competition. With this topic, the group will shift from examining oppositions within each individual to looking at oppositions within a group of individuals.

We compete with one another in school, in work, and even in our private relationships. There is nothing intrinsically bad or destructive about competition. However, competitiveness becomes objectionable when it prevents us from cooperating to achieve goals and desires. Some thinkers have claimed that competitiveness is deeply rooted in the very nature of human beings. It is difficult to know what such a claim means or whether an intended corollary is that the desire to cooperate is not equally deep. Certainly, the signs of competitiveness go as far back in our history as one wishes to go. Wars go as far back as any record. And every society or culture we know of has played games that entailed both victory and defeat. Even arguing a point that one believes to be true is laced with competitiveness. For example, the manner in which one refers to a text in a discussion can often be used competitively.

Conversely, we also have an abundance of historical evidence of complex forms of cooperation between people. Villages, common languages, corporations, and all forms of association are evidence of the need to move past our differences to pursue common goals. As our goals become more complex and our associations increasingly incorporate people of wide cultural diversity, our methods of cooperation must also shift to accommodate the increased pace and changeability of modern life. Thinking cooperatively requires one to recognize the limits of one's own approach and question whether there are definite right answers to complex problems, or if some answers are simply better or worse than others.

In Lessons 6, 7, and 8 the group considers the differences between competition and cooperation. In Lesson 6, competition is addressed in the text, as well as in the Individual and Small

Group Work, using the paragraphs that students wrote in Lesson 5. In Lesson 7, the topics will be approached through the text and an examination of the discussion process itself. In Lesson 8, the text and the Resolution Chart will be the vehicles.

In the text for Lesson 6, from *The Rhetoric*, Aristotle compares young men to old men. He states that young men have strong desires and are very trusting. They feel they know everything and wish to be honored. Above all else, young men love competition and victory. Old men, by contrast, are not certain about anything; they are suspicious instead of trusting, and fond of money instead of victory.

According to Aristotle, the one characteristic young and old men share is pity, although they feel pity for very different reasons. Pity takes a person out of oneself and connects him or her with others. Pity is different from cooperation, which also connects people, and it would be useful to ask the class whether and why they pity people. Do they pity people they defeat in a contest? Do they think the defeated person wants to be pitied?

What we see here is a combination of the attitudes that have come up in the last five meetings and how, if these attitudes and the goals they determine are pursued unchecked, they lead into their opposites. Since the students are involved in a competition today (on choosing a paragraph), it would be appropriate at some stage to ask how it feels to be picked, and how it feels to be overlooked.

Lesson Plan 6

1. INDIVIDUAL WORK...8 minutes
   - Ask the students to reread their paragraphs and complete the worksheet.

2. SMALL GROUP WORK...10 minutes
   - Divide the class into groups of five.
   - Have the students take turns reading their paragraphs aloud.
   - The small groups should choose the paragraph they believe to be the best.
   - They, as a group, should look over the paragraph again and rework it.

3. GROUPS REPORT ....10 minutes
   - Bring the groups back into the circle and ask a member of each group to read his or her group's paragraph to the class.
   - After all of the paragraphs have been read, have the class vote for the one they think is best.

4. TEXT...2 minutes
   - Read the text aloud as students follow along.
   - Give the students about thirty seconds to write down a question.

5. DISCUSSION..13 minutes
   - Using the random selection device that the students chose in Lesson 6, ask a student to read his or her opening question.

6. RESOLUTION CHART...2 minutes
   - Remind the students that the group will discuss their charts in Lesson 8.

Total: 45 minutes

Worksheet 6

Individual Work

Reread the paragraph you wrote at the end of Lesson 5.

   1. Of the items below, check the two that you consider the best features of your paragraph.

     a) _____ The idea that you expressed

     b) _____ The way you used language

     c) _____ The way it is organized

     d) _____ The examples you used

     e) _____ The reasons offered

   2. Check the two items that you consider the worst features of your paragraph.

     a) _____ The idea you expressed

     b) _____ The way you used language

     c) _____ The organization

     d) _____ The examples you used

     e) _____ The reasons offered

Small Group Work

   1. Have each member of your group read his or her paragraph aloud to the group.

   2. As a group, decide which paragraph is the best one in your group.

   3. Work together as a group to improve the paragraph you have chosen.

   4. Choose someone to read your group's paragraph aloud to the whole class.

Rhetoric
Aristotle

There are very great differences between young and old men. The young have strong desires, but these change very quickly. Their desires are very strong while they last, but are quickly over. The young often get angry. This is because they love honor and cannot stand being insulted. Therefore, they become furious when they imagine they have been treated unfairly. Yet, while young men love honor, they love victory even more, because they are eager to feel superior to others. And young men love both victory and honor more than money because they do not know what it's like to do without money. They look at the good side of everything because they haven't seen much wickedness. They are very trusting because they have rarely been cheated. All of their mistakes come from overdoing everything. Young men both love and hate too much. This is because they think they know everything and are sure of everything. If they hurt others, it is because they mean to insult them rather than harm them. They are always ready to pity others because they think everyone is basically honest. They judge their neighbors by their own harmless natures, and so can't believe that people deserve to be treated badly.

Old men are very different. They have often made mistakes and have been taken in many times. For them, life is bad business. The result of this is that they are sure about nothing, and so always under-do everything. They "think" but never claim to "know." Because they are hesitant about everything, they add a "possibly" or a "perhaps" to whatever they say. Their experience makes them suspicious, and they think that everything is worse than it appears. Old men are not generous because money is one of the things they need, and they have seen how hard it is to get, and how easy it is to lose. They lack confidence in the future partly because of the experience that most things go wrong and turn out worse than one expects. They live by memory rather than hope, for what is left to them of life is very little compared to what has passed. Old men are always talking about the past because they enjoy remembering it. Their anger is sudden but weak. They guide themselves by reason much more than by feeling, for reason is directed to what is useful; feeling to what is right. If they harm others it is because they want to injure them and not, as in the case of the young, to insult them. Both young and old men feel pity toward others. However, they feel pity for different reasons. Young men feel pity out of kindness. As was said, young men believe people are better than they really are and so don't deserve to be harmed. Old men, on the other hand, imagine that anything that happens to another might happen to them. And it is this possibility that stirs their pity.

Possible Questions to Raise

- Do you agree with Aristotle's comparison of old and young men? Why?
- What is the distinction between the two kinds of pity in the last paragraph?
- Do you think Aristotle was a young man or an old man when he wrote this? Why?
- Do you think it is true that young men love honor more than money? Why?

Failed Cooperation

One of the principal goals of the Touchstones program is that students learn the skills required to cooperate with others. We discover and rediscover the need to cooperate with others countless times during our lives, but all too often we forget the experience soon after. Moments of crisis, tragedy, and disaster often force us to confront the need to cooperate. Only when our ordinary, daily, habitual lives break down does the need to cooperate become visible and intense. In these moments of crisis, we also recognize our individual limits. Cooperating with others seems less necessary when our habits and the social organizations in which we play, learn, work, and live are operating smoothly.

In our current times, traditional forms of organization and institution are being redesigned and reformed more quickly than most people can adapt. Our societies need increasingly flexible and fluid structures and operations. As the workplace changes, so must our educational systems and methods, if they are to prepare future generations for the new workplace. Our educational system must arm our students with sets of generalized cooperative skills that enable them to work as members of flexible teams and carry many different roles and responsibilities. A variety of restructuring schemes are being developed in schools and school districts across the country to meet these new needs. The Touchstones program itself is intended to help meet that need on the level of the classroom—to help each group of students discover the need to cooperate and to build the skills necessary to maintain a high level of team effectiveness.

One of the necessary steps in learning to cooperate is examining one's strengths and weaknesses. Examining one's own behavior is much easier when one is interacting in a genuine way with other people. In this sort of interaction, each individual can see which of their qualities help cooperation, and which qualities hinder it. Individuals discover that they often mishear others, learn better ways of making themselves understood, and learn methods of making sure that they are heard. Individuals also learn that there are times when it is best to keep quiet, to help other members of the group gain the confidence to speak, that certain tones of voice or facial expressions can inadvertently shut other people down, or that a habitual way of speaking has the potential to offend. In Lesson 7, your students will explore their own strengths and weaknesses explicitly in the activities, and extend that exploration by discussing limitation.

The text for Lesson 7 is a tale of the Miwok people about a failed cooperative discussion. The discussion leader, the coyote, sets the group of animals a task about which very little is clear. A new animal—man—is to be created. The question is what he should be like. The animals are seated in a circle, just as in Touchstones, and are requested to discuss and decide this issue. However, they do not discuss and cooperate. Instead, each gives a short speech that is followed by a rebuttal from the next animal and a new proposal. Each animal thinks that man should be imbued with whatever quality the speaker believes to be his own strength. These assertions about strength require the next animal to point out that each animal's strength can also be a weakness. Finally, the discussion leader, the coyote, recognizes the failure of the attempt to cooperate, and by tricking them, forms a creature that is different from all of the animals. Worksheet 7 prepares students for the discussion by asking them about their own strengths and weaknesses. They will also complete a short writing exercise on the topic that should be kept private.

Lesson Plan 7

1. INDIVIDUAL WORK...15 minutes
   - Have the students fill out Worksheet 7 on strengths and weaknesses in discussions. The students are asked to order their strengths from 1 to 4. Greatest strength is number 1, least strength is number 4. Students should order their weakness the same way, with 1 as the greatest weakness, and 4 as the least.
   - Ask students to draw lines connecting strengths and weakness that they assigned the same number; they should connect their greatest strength to their greatest weakness, and so on.
   - Ask students to write a paragraph on Worksheet 7 about how they think their greatest strength might be related to their greatest weakness.
   - Students' answers should be kept private and will not be read or discussed in class.

2. TEXT..2 minutes
   - Use the randomizing device to determine who will ask the opening question.

3. DISCUSSION..25 minutes
   - After some discussion of the student's opening question, ask the group to consider why the animal discussion failed and how, if they were the coyote, they might have tried to get the animals to cooperate on this task.
   - At some point, you should ask them how they would have gotten the animals to approach the issue of strengths and weaknesses.

4. RESOLUTION CHARTS...10 minutes
   - Give students time to fill out their resolution charts.
   - Ask them to look through their journal entries and think about whether they have successfully kept their resolutions. In the next class they will discuss their results.

Total: 45 minutes

Worksheet 7

Individual Work

1. Listed below are four strengths and four weaknesses typical of participation in discussions. In the blanks next to the strengths, number your strengths from greatest (1) to least (4). Do the same for your weaknesses. When you finish, draw lines connecting the strengths and weaknesses that you gave the same number. Your greatest strength (1) should connect to your greatest weakness (1), second greatest strength (2) to second greatest weakness (2), etc.

Strengths in discussion	**Weaknesses in discussion**
___ I listen carefully to others.	___ I often talk to my neighbor
___ Others understand what I say	___ I only speak to certain other students
___ I don't interrupt.	___ I only speak when I'm sure about an answer
___ I read the text carefully.	___ I don't say what I really think.

2. Imagine that someone who knows you sees your list. That person notices the strength you numbered (1) and the weakness you numbered (1). After thinking about it for a bit, the person says. "It makes a lot of sense to me that you gave those two actions the same number because . . ."

Write a few sentences below that this person might say to explain why your greatest strength and greatest weakness might go together.

The Creation of Man
A Tale of the Miwok

When the coyote finished creating the world, he decided to create man. He called a council of all the animals. They met in an open space in the forest, and sat in a circle. The lion sat in the place of honor. On his left was the grizzly bear, then the brown bear, and then the others up to the mouse who sat next to the lion on his right side.

The lion spoke first. "This new creature, man, should have a terrible voice like me so he can frighten everyone. And he should have strong teeth, claws, and hair all over."

"That's ridiculous!" said the grizzly. "With a voice like yours, he would frighten the animals he was hunting. But he should have great strength and be able to move quickly and silently, like me."

"I agree, a terrible voice would be absurd," said the buck. "But man would look foolish if he didn't have antlers and sharp eyes like me."

"What if he travels through bushes?" asked the sheep. "If he had antlers, he would get caught. He needs horns, like me, rolled up on each side, and very strong."

The beaver now spoke. "Why are we talking about horns and antlers? He needs a tail, broad and flat like mine. Then he could haul mud and sand on it."

"And what about wings?" asked the owl. "Without wings, man would be useless."

"Wings!" shouted the mole. "With wings he'd bump against the sky. And with both wings and eyes, flying near the sun would burn out his eyes. But if he were blind like me, he could burrow in the soft, cool ground."

"Without eyes, how could he see what he's eating?" asked the mouse. So with all of these different opinions the council began arguing.

The coyote then spoke up. "You're all foolish. You're fighting now because you want man to be just like yourselves. We can make an animal better than any of us if we work together. He could have four legs, each with five fingers. He needs a strong voice, but shouldn't roar all the time. His feet should be like yours, Grizzly, and since the eyes of the buck are so good, man should have eyes like that. And the fish has no hair. And his claws should be as long as the eagle's so he could hold things in them. And he'll need to be cunning and crafty, so he should be like me."

The coyote thought since he had taken some part of each of them, the animals would agree. But no one was pleased. Each set to work accordingly to his ideas. Each animal took some earth and carved it just like himself, except the coyote. He made the kind of man he had talked about, a man who would be like all the animals but yet very different. Late that night, the animals stopped work and fell asleep. Only the coyote didn't stop, for he was crafty. He stayed up all night, hard at work, until he finished. Then he threw water on the other lumps of earth and destroyed the models of the other animals. In the morning he finished his own model and gave it life before the others woke up. So the coyote made man. He was unlike any of the animals but yet like all of them.

Possible Questions to Raise

- Why does the discussion between the animals fail?
- How would you have encouraged the animals to cooperate?
- How would you talk to the animals about their strengths and weaknesses?

Cooperation and Differences

It is often stated that in order to get along, people must have "something in common." People who have lived through a difficult and dangerous experience—a natural disaster, a war, a common type of loss, or a struggle with a specific illness or problem—find that they are more comfortable and open with others who have had the same experience. This phenomenon is so striking that sometimes people who do not know one another immediately trust one another as soon as they discover a commonality of experience, for instance when two citizens of the same country come across one another while traveling in a foreign place. This kind of shared commonality is often viewed as a necessary element of cooperation. As corporations become more flexible, many executives and managers are sent on weekend retreats in which they engage in activities designed to bring out such commonalities. The hope is that the team formed in that weekend will transfer certain attitudes back into the normal work environment.

Specific forms of cooperation already appear to exist in our society. Sports teams not only spend hours of practice time developing the individual skills of an athlete but also learning to work together as a team. Each athlete has certain strengths that are different from those of his or her teammates, and yet necessary for the team to perform well. The cooperation we are developing in Touchstones Discussions is more like that of an athletic team than it is like the kind of cooperation that is based on commonality. It is based on the recognition of a need to connect with diverse groups of people who do not necessarily share much in common. Participants who develop these skills can actively form themselves into a group, carry their skills from one group to another, and recognize that the distinction between insiders and outsiders becomes of no useful relevance. In fact, for the purposes of a group discussion, those who are least connected through common experiences, attitudes, and abilities, are most useful to one another.

In the last class, students individually tried to pinpoint their own strengths and weaknesses, and the interrelation between the two. In order for cooperation to move from cooperation *despite* differences to cooperation *through* differences, all students must recognize the need for different perspectives in discerning their personal strengths and weaknesses. Recognition of this need is a precondition for real cooperative thinking, cooperative learning, and cooperative action.

The first step is to notice that our strengths and weaknesses generally go together. Students often, and especially in school, misperceive themselves. They define themselves either by their strengths or by their weaknesses. However, strengths and weaknesses, as they develop in our society, very frequently go together. For example, articulate speaking rarely accompanies sensitive listening. But once this connection is recognized, it forces some students out of their complacency and gives others a self-respect they hadn't had. One purpose of participation in Touchstones is to teach students how to utilize their already existing intellectual strengths to work explicitly on correcting their weaknesses. Students can often develop a clearer picture of themselves through hearing how others view them. In this class, the students will explore how students who are quite different from one another can help one another discover which of their weaknesses need attention.

In Lesson 2, *The Autobiography of Benjamin Franklin*—the students were asked to devise a resolution for themselves on how to improve their behavior in Touchstones Discussions, and to keep a weekly record of their success or failure. It is now time to consider this record. In Lesson 8, the students are asked to suggest a resolution for each of the other two students in their group. They will also discuss their previous resolutions and whether they succeeded in keeping it.

The text by Goethe, *The Experiment*, addresses how, in scientific investigation, a scientist needs others in order to help him see more clearly. In his investigations, the scientist must take on a distance from his own likes and dislikes, his own habits and fears. For this task, Goethe claims we require people who are different from ourselves. He contrasts this situation with that of an artist or poet who should not listen to others' advice until he or she has completed the work. The exercise the students do in this lesson deals with the issues raised by Goethe. In Goethe's view, the students act as artists when they make their individual resolutions. But in the resolution they make today, they act more like scientists, who must take others' advice throughout the course of their investigations. They must choose a resolution for their improvement that is suggested by another person. Since the concern of the scientist is to eliminate his own likes and dislikes, his pleasures and pains, it is most useful to the scientist to have the assistance of people who do not share his own characteristics. In other words, people who do not know us very well are the most useful.

Lesson Plan 8

1. SMALL GROUP WORK...15 minutes
   - Ask one-third of your class to volunteer to be group selectors.
   - Ask each of these students to choose two other students. If the numbers don't work out, allow one or two groups to have four students.
   - Tell selectors to pick one student whom they know pretty well and one whom they do not know very well outside of class.
   - Ask the entire class whether the composition of the groups fits the criteria. If there are any objections to any of the groups, adjust accordingly.
   - Note: Depending on your class, this may be difficult, and you may have to make a few exceptions. It is nevertheless worthwhile to make the attempt.
   - Distribute Worksheet 8 to the students.
   - Have the students do the Small Group Work. Make it clear that students should not share with one another until they are ready to answer question 4.
   - Ask each student to report to the others on the resolution he or she made in Lesson 2 and on whether they succeeded in keeping it. Then each member of the group should tell the other members what resolutions he or she would suggest for each of them.

2. TEXT...2 minutes
   - Read the text aloud while students follow along silently.

3. DISCUSSION...15 minutes
   - Randomly select a student to ask the opening question.

4. INDIVIDUAL WORK...13 minutes
   - Ask students to complete the Individual Work.
   - Ask each student to mark an "S" on a scrap piece of paper if the person who they named in question 1 is the same person they named in question 2, or to mark a "D" if the person in question 2 is different from the person in question 1. Collect the papers before the students leave and tabulate the results before the next class.

Total: 45 minutes

Worksheet 8

Small Group Work

1. What was your resolution from your Resolution Chart in Lesson 2? Write a few sentences on how you tried to keep the resolution and whether you succeeded.

2. Write a resolution for improvement in Touchstones Discussions that you think each of the other two people in your group should make for the future. They might be the same, but they will probably be different.

Resolution for _____

_____

_____

_____

Resolution for _____

_____

_____

_____

3. Briefly describe how *you* would go about keeping each of the resolutions you suggested.

4. Write down the resolutions suggested to you by the other two students.

Suggested by _____
Resolution: _____

_____

_____

Suggested by _____
Resolution: _____

_____

_____

Individual Work

1. Of the two resolutions suggested by your group members, which one will you adopt?

2. Of the two other members of your group, whom do you know better?

3. Tear off a scrap of paper. If the person you named in question 2 is the person who suggested the resolution you picked in question 1, then write "S" for "same." If the person you named in question 2 is *not* the person who suggested the resolution you are adopting, write "D" for "different." Your teacher will collect these and tabulate the results for the next class.

The Experiment
Johann von Goethe

When we notice things around us, we relate them to ourselves. We like some of these things, and we dislike others. Some things attract or repel us; others help or harm us. This natural way of seeing things seems as easy as it is important, although it can lead to many errors. A far more difficult task arises when our thirst for knowledge makes us want to see how the objects in nature are in themselves and in relation to one another. Then we lose the yardstick we had earlier. We must get rid of the yardstick that we ourselves are. We must forget our own pleasure and pain, likes and dislikes, and whether something helps or harms us. We must be completely neutral. We must seek the truth about things, and not what pleases us. A true scientist must be unmoved by how beautiful or how useful a plant is. He must explore its shape and its relation to other plants.

If the scientist is to explore hidden relationships in nature, he must find his way in a world where he seems alone. He must not jump to conclusions, and yet he must keep his eye on the goal. He must criticize himself where no one else can test him. He must question himself even when he is most enthusiastic. Though this seems impossible, it must not stop us from doing what we can.

Many people are capable of sharp observation. When we show them things, they enjoy observing and have skill at it. When I discuss my interests with people who don't know much about what I'm doing, they often see what I didn't notice. They correct what I did too quickly or get beyond the habits and fears that hold me back. And what is true in so many human activities is also true in regard to science. The interest of many people focused on one thing can produce excellent results. A scientist will meet his downfall if he envies others or desires to work alone.

We should also realize that scientific discoveries are made not so much by particular people as by the age they live in. In fact, many scientists often make great discoveries at the same time. We saw how much we owe to and need the community and our friends. Now we discover our debt to the age of history we live in. In both cases, we can't say often enough how much we need communication with others and their help, their warnings and criticism, to hold us to the right path and help us along it.

So in science we must do exactly the opposite of what we do in art. An artist—a painter or a poet—should never show a work to the world before it is finished. This is because it is difficult for others to advise or help with it. However, once the poem or painting is finished, he must listen carefully to praise or criticism. He must make it a part of his own experience and prepare himself for new works. In science, it is very different. We must publish every piece of evidence, every idea. No scientific theory should be built until its plan and materials are widely known and judged.

Possible Questions to Raise

- Do you agree that an artist should not seek the advice of others until the work is completed?
- Imagine that you are a scientist and that you need to choose someone to help you avoid your own biases. How would you go about choosing this person? What characteristics would you look for in such a person?
- Why is it hard to be objective?
- Is it easier to hear criticism from someone you know or someone you don't know?
- What does Goethe mean when he says it is difficult to "see how the objects in nature are in themselves and in relation to one another?"
- When you have to make a decision, are you more likely to ask others for help or figure it out on your own?

Fairness and Weighing Evidence

In the last two classes, the students were asked to make decisions. In Lesson 7 they made a decision about their own strengths and weaknesses. In Lesson 8, they made a decision about two other people. In both cases, the students made judgments. They judged themselves, and they judged others. We all make judgments throughout our lives. We judge ourselves, we judge others, we judge what we do and do not want, and we judge what is important and what is unimportant. If we didn't make judgments, we would become paralyzed and would barely be able to live our lives. And yet we don't judge everything. Consider the following scenario, suggested by the eighteenth-century thinker David Hume: Imagine a person seated in a chair. What if each time he was about to get up, he had to judge whether the floor would hold him? Such a person would be paralyzed and unable to live his life. Thus, making judgments about everything, and never making judgments at all, lead to the same result.

A crucial part of making judgments is the consideration of the pieces of evidence on which judgments are based. Evidence can be good or bad, sufficient or insufficient. People are expected to use evidence when making judgments, rather than simple habit or whimsy. When they do make decisions by habit, we say that they have acted "without thinking."

In Touchstones, we have been creating a structure in which students can look at their intellectual habits, judge them, and experiment with new ones. Touchstones also creates a highly fluid environment, in which habits need to be examined, judged, and possibly replaced. We cannot prepare our students for life in modern society by developing only specific habits and skills that have a limited life span. Our students must practice judging their habits and determining when new habits are necessary. Evidence is one of the crucial factors in making judgments. Essential to the ability to judge evidence is the ability to see things for what they are and not what we want them to be. In our relationships with other people, this sort of objectivity is often called fairness. In today's class, the students will explore these issues. In the exercise, they will look at habits, judgments, and evidence. In the reading, they will consider the same concern in relation to fairness.

Since your first meeting, the discussion group will have fallen into certain patterns of behavior. As a group, your students may be uncomfortable with periods of silence; there may be side conversations; people may be speaking simultaneously; they may constantly argue with each other; certain students may dominate; many students may still look to you for approval or expect you to take the lead; some students might build on what others say; the discussion may have nothing to do with the text, or be too concerned with the text. All of these behaviors are potential habits. In Lesson 9, the students are asked to judge themselves as a class, determine how to evaluate their various judgments, and decide how to act on those judgments.

The text, *God, Death, and the Hungry Peasant*, also concerns fairness. A starving peasant steals a chicken and goes off into the hill with it. Forgetting the hunger of his family, he decides to cook the chicken for himself. In this action, he has broken his normal habits, which presumably involve caring for his wife and children, and has chosen to look after himself. While he cooks the chicken, two strangers approach and ask to share his food with him. The first is called God, but would perhaps more aptly be called Life, and the second is Death. He refuses the request made by God because God gives what he wants to people he likes, and withholds good from people he doesn't like. Certain people are given food, palaces, and horses, and others, like the peasant, are given nothing. From the perspective of the peasant, this is unfair. The second stranger—Death— is treated differently. The peasant shares his food with Death because he views Death as fair and just. Death treats everyone the same.

Lesson Plan 9

1. INDIVIDUAL WORK..5 minutes
    - Tell the students that all discussion groups have strengths and weaknesses, and that in Lesson 9 they will decide what their biggest problem is as a group.
    - Pass out Worksheet 9.
    - Ask the students to choose the two problems that most characterize their class. They should give the biggest problem five points and the second biggest problem three points.

2. REPORTS ON INDIVIDUAL WORK..15 minutes
    - Ask the students how their worksheets, the "evidence" for making the group judgment, should be used to determine the biggest problem for this group. A number of possibilities might be suggested: 1) The students might look only at the problems given five points and let each person contribute his or her choice. The problem that is selected most often is the group's most severe problem. 2) The students may ignore the points and count both the five-point and three-point problems equally, allowing the problem chosen the most to be the result. 3) The students can weigh the problems using the point system. The problem that receives the most points would be the one selected as the worst by the class. If students do not suggest these possibilities, you should bring them up.
    - Have the students vote for one method of counting the votes, and tabulate the results on the board.
    - Use the selected method to determine what the group's most severe problem.
    - After a decision has been reached, assign them to write a paragraph before the next Touchstones class about ways the class can improve on the selected issue.

3. TEXT...2 minutes
    - Read the text aloud and have students follow along silently.

4. DISCUSSION...23 minutes
    - Start the discussion by randomly selecting a student to pose the opening question.
    - Note: If the students focus too much on the fact that one stranger is called "God," suggest that they rename that stranger "Life." Then raise the question whether Life is unfair, and Death is fair.
    - At the end of class, remind the students to write a paragraph before the next class. Note: Emphasize that part of the next lesson depends on everyone having this assignment completed.

Total: 45 minutes

Worksheet 9

Individual Work

1. Of the following possibilities, choose the two that you feel characterize this discussion group as a whole. Give five points to what in your view is the biggest problem, and give three points to the next biggest problem.

    _____ a) We are uncomfortable with periods of silence.

    _____ b) There are too many side conversations.

    _____ c) We often speak at the same time.

    _____ d) We argue all the time.

    _____ e) Some people dominate the conversation.

    _____ f) We expect the teacher to run the discussions.

    _____ g) We don't build on what people say.

    _____ h) We talk too much about the text.

    _____ i) We don't talk enough about the text.

2. What would be the best method for counting up the results from question 1, in order to decide as a group what the biggest issue is?

Writing Assignment 9

Write a paragraph in your notebook about how the class should go about improving on the problem that the class voted was the biggest issue for your discussion group. These paragraphs will be used in the next Touchstones class.

God, Death, and the Hungry Peasant
A Tale from Mexico

Near Xoaxaca there lived a poor peasant. His farm was so small, and the soil so bad, that it never produced enough to feed his family. He, his wife and his children were always very hungry, even though he worked hard. For the last few weeks, he had to give up more and more of his own food to keep his family from starving.

One day, he stole a chicken. He thought he would go way up into the hills where he could cook it and eat it all by himself. He found a quiet spot in the hills where no one could see him, made a fire, put the chicken in a pot with some water from a stream, and cooked it. Just when the chicken was ready and he was about to eat, he saw a man coming along a footpath toward him. The peasant quickly hid the pot in some bushes.

The stranger greeted him.

"Hello, my friend. What are you doing here?"

"Nothing, señor. Just taking a rest. Where are you going?"

"I saw some smoke and came to ask you for something to eat," said the stranger.

"I haven't got anything, señor," replied the peasant.

"But you have a fire burning."

"Oh, this is just to keep myself warm," the peasant answered.

"I can smell chicken cooking," the stranger said. "You must have a pot hidden in those bushes."

"Well, yes, I have. But I'm not giving you any," the peasant complained. "I'm not even giving my wife and children any. I haven't eaten for many days, and this is all for me."

"Come, my friend," said the stranger. "Give me just a little piece. You don't know who I am."

The peasant answered, "I don't care who you are. I am not giving you any."

The stranger drew himself up and said, "You will when I tell you who I am."

"Well then, who are you?"

"I am the Lord, your God."

But the peasant cried out, "Now I'm certain I will never share my food with You. You're always bad to the poor people. You give palaces and horses and cattle and coaches and lots of food to the people You like, but to poor people like me You give nothing."

God tried to argue with him, but the peasant gave nothing to God. So He went away.

Just as the peasant was going to eat the chicken, a thin, pale man came along. "Good morning, my friend," said the stranger. "Please give me something to eat."

"No, señor, I won't."

"Don't be unfair. I'm also hungry. You can spare a little piece of that chicken."

"No! It's all for me," the peasant cried out.

"But you don't know who I am."

"God just left here because I wouldn't give Him any food. So who are you that says I'll give you some?"

"I am Death!"

Now the peasant smiled and said, "You are right. I'll give you some chicken because you are just and fair. You treat everyone the same—rich and poor, fat and thin, young and old. With you I will share the chicken."

Possible Questions to Raise

- Do you agree with the peasant's interpretation of God and Death?
- Is treating people differently always unfair?
- Is treating all people the same way fair?
- In general, do you think people are unfair to others on purpose or by accident?
- What kinds of evidence are most reliable?

Personal Strengths and Weaknesses

The class made a decision in the last meeting on what they as a group considered their most serious problem. In Lesson 9, the students first faced the need to determine their own goal as a group, analyze the problem, and act to correct it. In a Touchstones Discussion, there are two sets of habits that concern us: the habits of the individuals, and the habits of the group. Though modifying our individual habits is the principle and most difficult issue any of us face, the real difficulty may not be apparent to your students. Each of us believes a certain story about ourselves. We consider certain traits to be our strengths and others to be our weaknesses. But because we can only view ourselves from our own perspective, we often miss seeing habits that need to change. To glimpse what truly requires change involves taking a distance from our own perspectives on ourselves, and requires us to trust what others see in us.

Although trust plays a significant role in allowing us to reconfigure basic attitudes and habits, it can also be problematic and precarious. First, trust is not usually something we decide to have. Rather, is it something we feel or don't feel in respect to particular people. Second, trust can lead to dependence. Trusting someone to help us through the stages of a major change can often convince us to rely on that person rather than ourselves. And this clearly runs counter to the goals that we have for our students. We want them to take responsibility for their education and for changing their own habits. We want them to develop skills that enable them to take initiative in problem solving, intellectual exploration, and cooperation. Learning to make these changes requires more than blindly trusting others to tell us how we need to change. We must strike a balance between our own perspectives and the perspectives of others, between the text and our own voices, and between the group and the individual. Even in this initial stage we must look toward some sort of blending of all of these factors. This blending may, in fact, turn out to be the very result we are trying to achieve.

In Lesson 10, the final class of Unit I, the group explores the issue of trust, which previously came up in Lesson 5, *The Mortal Immortal*. In Lesson 9, the students had to determine what counts as evidence and how to weigh it. To prepare for Lesson 10, students were to write a paragraph on how the class can improve on the issue they selected in Lesson 9. Some of the students may not have done the assignment for a variety of reasons. Those who have not completed the assignment will have to complete it at the beginning of the class today. Since the students resolved to undertake to improve in whatever way decided in Lesson 9, each member of the group needs to feel that everyone in the group is committed to make the attempt to improve. Completing the paragraph clearly reflects the level of commitment to the group. You should feel free to mention these concerns to the class and allow some discussion of them before insisting that the paragraphs be written at the start of class. Make it clear that their commitment to the group and their reliance on one another to succeed is the major concern.

The text for Lesson 10 is the story of Abraham and Isaac from *The Bible*. In it, God asks Abraham to take his only son to Mt. Moriah to sacrifice him as a burnt offering. In the story, Abraham does what God asks him, but, instead of losing his son, he gains him back. This story raises the issue of trust in the most vivid possible form. In the story, God is testing Abraham, and this request—to sacrifice his son Isaac—is the most extreme test. However, somehow Abraham is able to pass the test. It appears from the story that Abraham trusts God in spite of what he is asked to do.

Abraham's relationship to Isaac is not all that dissimilar from our relationship with our habits and attitudes. Parents often see their role in the world, both in terms of what they do and what they desire, as immediately connected with their children. For parents, children constitute one of the most important aspects of their world. Any change at all in their relationship—for better or worse—causes a serious change in some other part of life. Abraham is asked by God to change this world fundamentally; much as we are when we consider changing habits or strengths that we feel make us what we are. Before the discussion, remind the class that they are trying to implement the joint resolution on which they all agreed in the last class.

Lesson Plan 10

1. PARAGRAPHS..5 minutes
   - If some students have not completed their paragraphs, have those students write the paragraph now. While they are doing this, have the rest of the class quietly remain in their seats until those students have finished. The students who have done their paragraphs should sit silently in their seats and wait.
   - Note: This response may seem harsh on those who did the assignment, but it is necessary to make it clear that the class cannot continue until everyone can trust all the others to do what is expected, especially since in the next unit of classes the students will be asked to write before each class.

2. SMALL GROUP WORK...10 minutes
   - Divide the class into groups of five.
   - Have the students read their paragraphs aloud to one another.
   - After hearing each paragraph, the group should decide how to express the main point of each paragraph in one sentence, and have one student act as secretary to record the sentences.
   - Bring the groups back into the circle, and ask the secretaries to read the summary sentences.
   - Ask the entire group if they agree or disagree with the strategies and suggestions proposed.
   - As the students discuss strategies, point out to them that in some cases, these problems might also be strengths, for instance, if the group as a whole doesn't talk about the text enough, there might be individual students who do talk about the text quite often.
   - Point out, if the students don't realize it, that the issue of how they change as a group is quite different from how they may change as individuals. This is a very complex concern and you should not expect that it can be more than briefly mentioned today.

3. TEXT ....2 minutes
   - Read the text aloud and have students follow along.

4. DISCUSSION..23 minutes
   - Randomly choose a student to ask the opening question.

5. WRITING ASSIGNMENT ....5 minutes
   - Distribute Writing Assignment 11 to the students.
   - The students are asked to imagine themselves to be artists who will paint the scene of Abraham and Isaac on Mt. Moriah, which is described in the fourth paragraph of the Genesis text, and reprinted on Writing Assignment 11. Ask the students to write a paragraph describing how their painting would look. They should bring their paragraphs to the next Touchstones class.

Total: 45 minutes

Genesis: Chapter 22
The Bible

God put his servant Abraham to a test. "Abraham, Abraham," He called. "Here I am," replied Abraham. "Take your son," God said, "your one and only child Isaac, whom you love, and travel to the land of Moriah. On a mountain that I will show you, you must kill him and burn the body as an offering to me."

Abraham got up early the next morning. He saddled his donkey and took two servants and his son Isaac with him. He chopped the wood for the sacrifice and set off to the place God had pointed out to him. On the third day, Abraham saw the place. He said to his servants, "Stay here with the donkey. The boy and I will go on, we will worship and then return."

Abraham took the wood and loaded it on Isaac. With his own hands he carried the fire-stick and the knife. As they traveled, Isaac spoke to his father Abraham. "Father, we have the fire and the wood, but where is the lamb for the burnt offering?" Abraham answered, "My son, God himself will provide a lamb for the sacrifice." Then the two of them went on together.

When they had climbed the mountain God had shown him, Abraham built an altar and arranged the wood for the fire. Then he took and tied up his son Isaac. He put the child on the altar on top of the wood. Abraham stretched out his hand and seized the knife to kill his son.

But an angel of God called him, "Abraham, Abraham."

"Here I am," he said.

"Do not raise your hand, do not harm the boy," said the angel. "Now I know you fear God because you have not refused to sacrifice your only son."

Then Abraham looked up and saw a ram caught in a bush. He took the ram and offered it up as a sacrifice in place of his son Isaac.

The angel called Abraham a second time from heaven. "I swear because you were ready to offer up your only son, God will shower his blessings on you. Your descendants will be as many as the stars in the sky or the grains of sand on the shore. Your descendants will conquer their enemies, and they will be a blessing to all the nations of the world. This will be the reward for your obedience."

Possible Questions to Raise

- How would you be different if you suddenly lost what you believe to be your greatest strength?
- Why does Abraham trust God?
- Why is it difficult to trust people we don't know very well?
- What makes you trust someone you are meeting for the first time?
- In general, do you trust people until you are given a reason not to trust them? Or are you suspicious of people until you are given evidence that they can be trusted?

Writing and Writer's Block

Using a text from Paul Gauguin's journal, the students will explore why some people are afraid of writing and the nature of a writing block. They will investigate how the judgment of a reader can generate fears about having nothing to say. This will occur through contrasting writing for oneself in a journal or diary with writing for others. The student's writing assignment for this class is for their personal journal, so they will have had the experience of writing exclusively for themselves. Since exploratory writing is also primarily writing for oneself, journal and diary writing is a useful topic and an appropriate place to start.

In the text for Lesson 11, Gauguin compares painting with music and literature and argues that it is the most beautiful of the arts. Painting, according to Gauguin, allows the viewer to create a story or a dream, unlike literature in which the reader is a slave to the author's thoughts. This claim about literature should come up for discussion, since clearly the success of the writer depends on the reader's willingness to read. Uncertainty concerning the reader's willingness to read one's work can also cause a writer to fear writing—a fear usually called writer's block. But is this is equally true of painting and music? Painting, Gauguin claims, unlike music and writing, allows the viewer to appreciate its unity all at once. Literature and music are more linear, and occur over time. Readers are required to remember what has occurred previously if they are to appreciate the work as a whole. According to Gauguin, this requirement weakens the effect of the other two media. He claim that music is the least powerful of the arts. These claims are surprising because many people would consider music and literature more powerful than painting. In fact, lots of people find it difficult to respond to paintings. Gauguin addresses the difficulty by making the further claim that the only people who respond to paintings are those who are born to it.

You might ask the students if they agree with Gauguin's claims about painting. Considering whether some people understand or respond to particular subjects because of an inborn ability can open the way to a discussion about the differences between all of our various skills and abilities. You might also ask which of the three is the most personal or private form of artistic expression, and which is most public. Does a painter, for instance, expose himself in a way the writer or musician does not? Since writing will play an important role in the work of this unit, the text provides the students an opportunity to discuss their attitudes toward it in an indirect way.

For today's class, the students are supposed to come with their paragraphs. In their paragraphs, they are to imagine they are artists who intend to paint the scene of Abraham and Isaac, and describe how they would imagine the scene. The issue the class must again confront is whether everyone has in fact completed a paragraph. If everyone has written the paragraph you can move right away to the Individual Work. If some students have not completed paragraphs, you and the class will need to face this issue. In Lesson 10, you handled the situation somewhat punitively. In Lesson 11, the issue should be opened for discussion. It is likely that some students didn't complete paragraphs because they never do homework, or because they do not want to make the extra effort. Others may not have done it because of a fear of writing. For today's class you should assume, even if it is not wholly true, that the fear of writing is the reason that any of the students neglected to write a paragraph. Ask the class why they think some students didn't do the writing and encourage them to consider that some people may be afraid to write. This is both the issue the class needs to consider as well as a convenient way out for those who refused for other reasons. Finally, tell the students that the completion of their notebooks and worksheets is the admission ticket for participation in Touchstones from now on, and that you will decide what a student who has not completed the assignment must do instead of Touchstones.

Lesson Plan 11

1. WORKSHEET..6 minutes
   - Have students complete Worksheet 11.

2. SMALL GROUP WORK..8 minutes
   - Divide the class into groups of students who had the same answers to question 2.
   - Students collaborate on an explanation for their choice.

3. TEXT...2 minutes
   - Read the text aloud and ask students to write down an opening question.

4. DISCUSSION...25 minutes
   - Invite the students to share their answers to the worksheets, particularly questions 2 and 3.
   - After the students have shared, use the randomizing device to select a student to pose the opening question.
   - Encourage the group to consider the differences between writing in a journal for oneself and writing for others.

5. DISTRIBUTE WORKSHEET AND WRITING ASSIGNMENT..4 minutes
   - Ask the students to complete the Worksheet 12 and Writing Assignment 12 before the next class. Their paragraphs should be kept in their notebooks.

Total: 45 minutes

Worksheet 11

Individual Work

For today's class you wrote a paragraph describing what a painting of Abraham and Isaac on the mountain would look like. Choose the answer that best describes your thoughts while you were doing the assignment.

1. When you wrote your paragraph did you imagine other people reading it? If so, who?

2. People often think that it's easier to write in a journal or diary than to write for others. Why do you think they feel this?

   a) They are afraid other people won't understand them.
   b) They are afraid they have nothing to write.
   c) They are afraid other people won't be interested.

3. Which of the three items listed in question 2 is your greatest concern? Explain how this affects your writing.

Writing Assignment 11

Imagine that you are an artist and you plan to paint a picture based on the scene described in the passage below. Before the next Touchstones class, write a paragraph describing what your painting would look like. Some things you might consider: Would you show both Abraham and Isaac? Would you choose bright or dark colors? Would it be a clear or cloudy day? What kind of expressions would be on the faces if you decide to show the faces? Feel free to include whatever else you feel is appropriate.

"When they had climbed the mountain God had shown him, Abraham built an altar and arranged the wood for the fire. Then he took and tied up his son Isaac. He put the child on the altar on top of the wood. Abraham stretched out his hand and seized the knife to kill his son."

The Notebook
Paul Gauguin

Painting is the most beautiful of all the arts. All your sensations are brought together in it. When you stand in front of a painting, looking and thinking, you can create a story in your imagination of whatever you want, and have your soul caught up in deep memories. There is no effort of remembering—it just comes to you. Painting is a complete art, that adds all the other arts together and completes the senses. Harmonies of colors correspond to harmonies of sounds. Furthermore, in painting, a unity is obtained that is not possible in music, where tones and chords follow one another so that it takes effort if you want to connect the end with the beginning. In this regard, the eye is actually better than the ear. Hearing can only grasp a single sound at a time, but sight can take in everything it sees all at once, analyze it, and put it together again just as it wants.

Like literature, the art of painting tells us whatever it wants, but painting has the advantage of showing us the beginning, middle, and end all at once. Literature and music require us to make an effort of memory to appreciate the whole work. Because of this, music is the least powerful of the arts. You are free to dream when you listen to music; but you are equally free when you look at a painting. However, when you read a book, you are a slave of the author's thoughts. The author "talks" to the readers' minds, and we all know that reasoned-out feelings have no strength or power. Sight alone produces an immediate instantaneous response. It takes intelligence and knowledge to judge a book, but to judge a painting requires yet more than these. In a word, one has to be born to appreciate painting, and few are chosen among all those who are called.

Possible Questions to Raise

- What do you think is the most beautiful or powerful form of art?
- Why do you think Gauguin says that one must be born to appreciate art?
- What does Gauguin mean when he says, "we all know that reasoned-out feelings have no strength or power"? Do you agree?
- What are the differences between writing in a journal for oneself and writing for others?
- Why is journal writing easier than writing for other people?
- Could writing in a journal help people overcome their fears of writing?
- Do you agree with the statement "when you read a book, you are a slave of the author's thoughts"?
- What should a writer and a reader expect from one another?

Writing for an Audience

In Lesson 12, the students use a letter written to a friend by Helisenne de Crenne to explore the role of the reader. The reader first appears on the scene as someone we know and not as an anonymous person. The reader appears as the recipient of a letter. Students will consider what they as letter-writers expect from a reader. They will investigate why they write or might write letters. They will discuss components of letter writing as writing in which the writer has something to communicate to a reader, but also consider the exploratory aspect of the exchange, in that the reader's response to a text is to engage in the activity of writing.

In Lesson 12, the role of the reader will come more clearly into the picture than it did in Lesson 11, which concerned journal writing. What the students will consider in greater detail is the writing model that dictates that one only writes when one has something to communicate to potential readers.

Journal writing, which the students are doing for this class, will eventually form the model for exploratory writing. In keeping a journal or a diary we write for ourselves. The reasons for doing this are various and might have been discussed in the last class. But in most of these instances we, as writers, are the primary readers even if we sometimes imagine that others will read our journals or if while writing, we never plan to read what we have written. The simplest form in which a specific reader appears on the scene is in the case of letter writing. All of us, your students included, have written letters, even if they were no more than notes in class. You might bring up electronic communication, such as email, instant messaging, and text messaging, as a modern comparison to the formal letter writing displayed in the text.

The text for today's class is a letter written by a woman in medieval times, Helisenne de Crenne, to a friend. She confesses that she is in love and talks about the pain that being in love is causing her. She writes to her friend hoping that sharing her thoughts will bring relief to her pain. Her friend has been in love and so will understand what she feels. The situation is complicated by the fact that the writer had previously criticized this friend for the very feeling she herself now has. She is hopeful that her friend's understanding can ease her pain, but de Crenne is also afraid that her friend may return her previous criticism. De Crenne's relationship with the man she loves is quite similar to her friend's; she hopes to gain his love but is tormented by jealousy. This is made worse by the fact that she cannot speak with her lover. The memory of her friend's experience initially helps her. Her friend gained the man she loved and this gives de Crenne hope. Unfortunately, this hope increases her desire and consequently her pain. So what appeared to be a possible aid simply makes the situation worse. In order to break out of this cycle, de Crenne writes a letter but then runs the risk that her previous criticism will come back to haunt her.

In preparation for today's class, students will explore writing to a particular reader by making decisions in a similar situation. They will be asked to decide what they might put in such a letter and the reasons for writing it. In the discussion, students should compare their answers on the Worksheet 12 with the reasons and methods in Helisenne de Crenne's letter.

Lesson Plan 12

1. REVIEW INDIVIDUAL WORK..17 minutes
   - Ask students to report, by a show of hands, how they answered all parts of question 1. Tally their answers on the board. Ask some students to explain their answers.
   - Again through a show of hands, tally student responses to question 2. Ask them to give reasons for their answers. Allow some discussion if time permits.

2. TEXT..2 minutes
   - Read the text aloud and have students write an opening question.

3. DISCUSSION..22 minutes
   - Randomly select a student to ask the opening question.
   - Note: If students do not refer to their responses to question 3, you should ask for responses

4. DISTRIBUTE WRITING ASSIGNMENT 13..4 minutes
   - Ask the students to complete the assignment before the next class. The paragraphs are to be kept in their notebooks.

Total: 45 minutes

Worksheet 12

Individual Work

1. People write letters to friends for many reasons. Rank the reasons that would prompt you to write on a scale of 1to 4 (1 is most important, 4 is least important).

    _____ To tell your friend what's been happening to you.

    _____ To think about your friend while writing

    _____ To receive a letter from your friend.

    _____ To get your friend to think about you.

    Explain your choice briefly.

2. Imagine that a friend once did something of which you strongly disapproved, and you criticized your friend. Now you find you have done a very similar thing, and you want to write a letter to that friend about what you have done. Circle your answer to show how you would approach such a letter.

    Would you remind your friend that you criticized him or her?
    yes   no

    Would you apologize for how critical you were?
    yes   no

    Would you ask your friend for advice?
    yes   no

Which of the reasons best describes why you might write such a letter?

    a) To show your friend that you are honest by admitting what you did.
    b) To feel better by sharing with someone who has experienced something similar.
    c) To help yourself think about what you did by writing about it.
    d) To avoid having your friend find out from someone else.

Writing Assignment 12

After you have answered question 2, write the first paragraph of the imaginary letter in your notebook. Make sure your paragraph illustrates your answers from question 2. For instance, if you circled "yes" for the first question, make sure that in your paragraph you remind your imaginary friend about the time you criticized him or her. Bring your notebook to the next class.

Letter to a Friend
Helisenne de Crenne

When I first considered writing my secret thoughts to you, I hesitated. I remember warning and criticizing you about what now upsets and troubles me. And I was afraid you would criticize me in turn. So I planned to hide my pain. But concealed pains just grow worse, and I write now hoping that sharing my thoughts with you will bring some relief for my pain.

I'm not sure what to call the pain I am suffering. If I say my heart has been hit by Cupid's arrow, my heart will answer back that I let that happen. And we should listen to this reply. For, if our hearts were really pierced by an arrow, as we say, we would all die immediately. Where then is this pain that I feel? My body feels no pain, so the pain must be located somewhere in my mind. My mind is filled with troubling fantasies, and it is my mind that fills my heart with an incurable suffering. But why should I tell you these things? Haven't you felt them yourself?

Instead, I should tell you what troubles me. When I think about this matter, I realize I must not complain about love or about the man I love. He is handsome, modest, graceful and gentle, and all these qualities are signs that he will be faithful. But from somewhere, who knows where, a terrible feeling has settled on me. Like a witch, this feeling has stirred up in me a hateful jealousy. And this jealousy has created the haunting image of an ugly wicked old woman who shakes constantly like a leaf on a tree. The name of this horrible old hag is Fear. She torments me beyond life. To fight Fear and push her away, there appears in my mind the image of an old man, with a happy friendly face, and he speaks pleasant words to me. His name is Hope. He tells me to take courage and his persistence has helped. I keep saying to him, "Hope, defender of those who fear, do not leave me. Without you, I cannot survive my daily fears and pain."

My dear sweet friend, even if my greatest torment were only that I couldn't speak to the man I long for, my pain should not be taken lightly. The only thing that gives me hope is that you yourself finally got the man that you desired. But this thought makes my love and pain ever greater for as hope grows so does desire. You're probably thinking, "This woman, who thought she could not only defeat love but destroy it, has now herself been conquered." Don't be surprised. Fresh green wood is, at first, hard to burn but once it catches fire, it burns longer and with a more intense heat. I too have been tempted and excited by love. In the past, I was undefeated, but one day I was overtaken by it and today no woman is more in love than I am.

Possible Questions to Raise

- Is it harder to talk to someone or write to him or her about love? Why? About fear? About hope?
- When do you write notes, email, or letters instead of talking to people?
- What are the differences between writing a note, an email, an instant message, or a letter?

Similarities Between the Writer and the Reader

In Lesson 13, the students will further consider the relationship between the writer and the reader. Writers often write for other people, rather than for themselves. The perspective of the reader is therefore a crucial element in the writing. Using Ptolemy's text on astronomy, The Almagest, the students will look at a situation in which the writer and reader fundamentally agree on certain things—this agreement is then used by the writer as the basis from which to persuade the reader by argument or rhetoric.

Constructing a persuasive argument involves two components—what to say and how to say it. The content—the "what"—comes from the writer, while the "how" is determined by the writer's understanding of the reader. If the writer and reader have similar beliefs or perspectives, the writer can utilize reason, attempting to show that what the writer presents is simply an extension of what the reader already believes. If the reader's viewpoint is not compatible, then another path must be found. The reader may have a neutral viewpoint, neither agreeing nor disagreeing with the writer's perspective, or the reader may have an opposing one. The opposing perspective is the most difficult and, perhaps, important case and will be addressed in Lesson 14. In writing to persuade a neutral reader, the writer will generally identify where he or she and the reader do have commonalities. This task, which can be very complex, involves spelling out the shared beliefs or goals so the reader can recognize them as his or her own, and clarifying the nature of the connection between these and what the writer wishes the reader to accept. We will see this approach in today's text.

The text from Ptolemy's *Almagest* is the introduction to his work on astronomy. It is a kind of advertisement to show a reader the importance of studying this area of mathematics. Ptolemy's readers, like many of us, would probably prefer to study things other than mathematics, either because these things are more important or more useful. If mathematics were recognized as the most important or most useful subject to study, it would be much easier to convince people to do it.

The strategy Ptolemy uses can be examined without passionate commitment to the content of the text, since few of your students will have passionate feelings about learning astronomy. In the worksheet, the students are asked to think about issues of persuasion by deciding which activity they consider important, and then thinking about how they would convince two people to get involved in that activity. One person is to be someone they know well; the other, someone they do not know at all. Thus, they must examine how writing persuasively depends on the person to be persuaded.

In the Small Group Work today, students will compare their worksheets and offer suggestions to one another on their strategies. In the large group discussion, encourage students to explore and describe the strategy that Ptolemy uses in his argument. Encourage the group to explore ways of persuading someone of whatever they bring up.

Lesson Plan 13

1. REVIEW PARAGRAPHS..10 minutes
   - Have two student volunteers read both of their paragraphs.
   - Have students discuss the differences between the paragraphs and the different ways they tried to persuade the readers.

2. SMALL GROUP WORK..10 minutes
   - Have groups share their worksheet responses and offer one another advice on the best way to persuade both people they know and don't know.

3. TEXT..2 minutes
   - Read text aloud and have students write an opening question.

4. DISCUSSION..19 minutes
   - Randomly pick a student to ask their opening question.
   - Note: Try to keep students focused on methods of persuasion and not astronomy and physics.

5. WRITING ASSIGNMENT..4 minutes
   - Distribute Writing Assignment 14 and Worksheet 14

Total: 45 minutes

Worksheet 13

Most, if not all of us, spend time on one activity we feel is very important to us, such as sports, listening to music, studying, watching TV, making certain kinds of things, spending time with friends, playing music, painting, or writing.

1. Which of the activities you enjoy is most important to you?

2. The following are reasons why you might consider the activity important. On a scale of 1-10 (1 is least important and 10 is most important) rate these reasons along with one of your own.

_____ a) It is fun.

_____ b) I feel better about myself.

_____ c) It teaches me about the world.

_____ d) It teaches me about other people.

_____ e) It can help me achieve my goals.

_____ f) It makes me a better person.

_____ g) _____

3. Suppose you were trying to convince your closest friend to spend time on the same activity. Which two reasons would you use?

a) _____

b) _____

4. Suppose you were trying to convince someone whom you didn't know to spend time on this activity. In other words, imagine you are writing a commercial or advertisement about this activity for TV. What would you say to convince someone in the viewing audience to spend time on this activity?

Writing Assignment 13

1. In your notebooks, write one paragraph in which you try to convince your closest friend to do your favorite activity.

2. Write another paragraph in which you try to convince someone whom you don't know to do your favorite activity.

The Almagest
Ptolemy

True philosophers separate the theoretical kind of knowledge from the practical kind. For even if practical knowledge was theoretical before it became practical, there is still a great difference between them. This difference is shown by the fact that ordinary, uneducated people understand practical things, like morals and agriculture; whereas you have to study a great deal to understand theoretical subjects like mathematics. Also, to learn morals and farming you actually have to do something in the world. However, theory is learned by thinking carefully and systematically, and action in the world is unnecessary. But, even in practical matters, there is much of theoretical knowledge to be learned that is beautiful and has value. I have therefore trained myself to be on the look out for these particular practical things, and I especially look for those that can be given a mathematical form.

The theoretical kind of knowledge is properly divided into three parts: theology, physics, and mathematics. For, all things in the world are in motion, and all have a particular shape, and all are composed of matter. But, motion, shapes, and matter cannot themselves be seen. They can only be thought about. Therefore, the science that seeks for the original cause of motion, matter, and shape in the universe is looking for something that cannot be seen but only thought about. The original cause of motion, matter, and shape cannot itself be any of those things. The cause of them is God, and the theoretical science that seeks after God is called Theology. There is also a theoretical science that seeks to understand the particular properties of things, such as their color and texture, which can be experienced through the senses. This science is called physics, and the objects it studies are always changing, unlike God who is always the same.

There is also a third theoretical science which studies particular shapes and motions. This science tries to understand shapes and motions in terms of number. This is called mathematics. Mathematics is sort of in-between theology and physics because the things it studies, like numbers and shapes, can be experienced both through the senses, like physics, and through thought, like God. A triangle, for example, can be experienced as the shape of something, or as an object of thought on its own. Astronomy is a mathematical science, because it studies primarily the motions of the stars and planets in terms of number.

Finally, I noticed that both theology and physics give us only guesses, and not knowledge. In the case of theology, this is because the nature of God cannot be directly experienced. In the case of physics, this is because the properties of things change all the time in ways that are uncertain. Therefore, it is hard for people to agree about either theology or physics. However, mathematics does give trustworthy knowledge that results from methods everybody understands and agrees upon. I therefore decided it was the science most worthy of studying, not because it was about the most important thing, which is God, or because it was about the things of most immediate concern to us, which are material objects, but because it was about things we can know most clearly and with most certainty—numbers.

Possible Questions to Raise

- What things are the hardest to change someone's mind about?
- What sort of people do you think would be convinced by Ptolemy's argument?
- Why don't people like to change their minds about certain things?
- How do you react when someone tries to change your mind about something you believe?
- How would Ptolemy's strategies need to change to address a contemporary audience?
- What reasons might persuade you to study astronomy?

Differences Between the Writer and the Reader

Using a text opposing slavery and written by a former slave, the students will consider the difficult task of writing persuasively for readers who have fundamental differences from the writer. These differences can be of beliefs, presuppositions, and desires. In the case of a difference of beliefs, writing can play a crucial role in helping students learn to scrutinize their own perspectives in order to enlarge and even modify them.

Most people are willing to admit in a general way that some of their beliefs, opinions, and even points of view on their lives, the world, and others sometimes require modification. However, though many acknowledge this in an abstract way, acknowledging it in regard to specific views is much more difficult. In this lesson, students will examine some of their views and practice writing in order to change another person's point of view.

When the writer and reader are similar, as in Lesson 13, the writer is able to appeal to the shared beliefs and work upward from there. But when those fundamental beliefs are not shared, the writer needs to give the reader certain things: 1) the necessary distance from which to view his or her beliefs somewhat objectively, 2) the encouragement to examine those beliefs, and 3) the privacy necessary to be comfortable changing them if he or she chooses. When someone tries to change our minds about our deepest opinions, the result is often resistance, conflict, and argument. The writer must take care to address and overcome these potential tensions in the writing.

The students can begin to appreciate the problems of the writer and reader with conflicting perspectives by considering the piece by Olaudah Equiano. Equiano was a slave who wrote an account of his own life and tried to convince his readers that slavery is wrong. Though the writer has direct experience of slavery from the perspective of the slave, his readers do not, and most could not ever have such a perspective. His readers, on the whole, would be free people who have heard about slavery, observed aspects of slavery, or are themselves slave owners. Equiano understands that his readers are possible participants in the institution of slavery.

The position of Equiano is completely different from the positions of the writers of the previous two texts. In Lesson 12, Helisenne de Crenne was writing to a friend who has previously had the very experience of love she herself was describing. In Lesson 14, Ptolemy could appeal to beliefs that are shared by all of his readers. Equiano has neither of these approaches available to him. Therefore, Equiano cannot begin with the experience of the slave. Instead, he starts with what is knowable or imaginable to his readers: a description of slave traders and slave owners and how what they do changes them. Then he describes the institution of slavery and the relationship that the master and the slave have with one another. It is only after going through these two steps, each of which is accessible to his readers' imaginations, that he describes the situation of the slave; a situation his readers would only know from distant observation.

When Equiano does approach the situation of the slave, he does so through the slave owner's motive for slavery—greed. He argues that by taking on this kind of power to satisfy his greed, the slave owner defeats his own purpose. Instead of the gains he desires, he creates a model for the slave to imitate in which they become dishonest, cruel, and in a perpetual state of war with their owners. By stating that the slave owner harms himself and works against his own self-interest, Equiano tries to persuade his readers to agree with his own view—that slavery is wrong.

We, as readers of this text, are very different from the readers for whom this text was written. Few of us need to be convinced that slavery is wrong. However, all of us experience the relationship of which slavery is the most extreme form—the relationship of one person having some sort of power over another. Often this relationship is both useful and necessary to the two people involved, whereas the extreme form described in today's text is useful to neither person. One question that emerges is in what ways the useful relationships of power are similar and dissimilar from the most extreme form, and how to make sure the useful varieties do not move too far in the direction of what Equiano describes. In the worksheet, the students are asked to think about this question. They must rank relationships and experiences in terms of the degree of power in each. They must write reasons the feeling of power can be either beneficial or harmful. These questions are preliminary to the crucial one, which asks them to imagine they are the readers who must be persuaded and to decide which kinds of writers would most likely persuade them.

Lesson Plan 14

1. SMALL GROUP WORK...7 minutes
   - Divide the class into groups of five students. Groups are to compare and discuss their answers to questions 1 and 2 from the worksheet and decide which relationship in question 1 has the greatest power.

2. REVIEW WORKSHEET...5 minutes
   - In the large group, have volunteers share responses to questions 3 and 4.

3. DISCUSSION...5 minutes
   - Have students volunteer responses to question 5 and have the class discuss the two possibilities briefly before moving to the text.

4. TEXT...2 minutes
   - Before reading the text, tell the class it was written by an ex-slave and read by free people, some of whom would be involved in owning or trading slaves.
   - Read the text aloud and have students write an opening question.

5. DISCUSSION...25 minutes
   - Randomly select a student to ask the opening question.

6. WRITING ASSIGNMENT...1 minute
   - Distribute Writing Assignment and Worksheet 15

Total: 45 minutes

Worksheet 14

1. Who has the most power over your life? Certain people carry certain degrees of power in everyone's life. Rank the relationships in the list below from 1 to 6 (1 means "has the most power" and 6 means "has the least power").

    _____ Older brother/sister over their younger sibling

    _____ Policeman over a citizen

    _____ Parent over a child

    _____ Teacher over a student

    _____ Senior over a freshman

    _____ Writer over a reader

2. Certain situations give us a feeling of power. Rank the situations below from 1 to 6 (1 makes you feel the most powerful and 6 doesn't make you feel powerful).

    _____ Knowing a secret

    _____ Winning a game

    _____ Winning an argument

    _____ Getting a perfect score on a test

    _____ Performing an activity well, like a jump shot, a piece of music, or a dance

    _____ Disobeying a parent or teacher

3. List two reasons the feeling of power could be beneficial.

4. List two reasons the feeling of power could be harmful.

5. Imagine that you own slaves and someone is trying to convince you to free them. Who would be more convincing to you? A person who has owned slaves and freed them, or a person who was once a slave? Choose one and explain why.

Writing Assignment 14

In your notebook, write a paragraph in which you persuade slaveholders that slavery is wrong.

The Interesting Narrative of the Life of Olaudah Equiano
Olaudah Equiano

These practices were not confined to particular places or individuals. In all the different islands in which I have been (and I have visited no less than fifteen), the treatment of slaves has been nearly the same. Indeed, the history of slavery in one island or even on one plantation might well serve as a history for the whole practice. The slave trade destroys men's minds and hardens them to every feeling of humanity. For I refuse to believe that the dealers in slaves are born worse than other men. No, it is the result of this mistaken greed that it corrupts the milk of human kindness and turns it into bitter gall. Had these men pursued different activities they might have been as generous, as tenderhearted, and as just as they are now unfeeling, greedy, and cruel. Surely, this trade in slaves cannot be good. It spreads like a disease and changes everything it touches. It violates the first natural rights of mankind—equality and independence.

The practice of slavery gives one man a rule and a dominion over his fellow men that God could never have intended. It raises the slave-owner to a state far above a human being, for it forces the slave into a position below it. One pretends to be a god, the other is made an animal. Through the arrogance of human pride it places a difference between them that is immeasurable in distance and endless in time. Yet how mistaken and self-defeating is even the owner's greed! Are slaves more useful by being made animals than they would be if they were allowed to be men? When you make men slaves, you take away half of their virtue and ability. And by your own action you set for them the example of fraud, rape, and cruelty. You force them to live in a state of war with you, and then you complain that they are not honest or faithful. You beat them; you keep them ignorant; and then you claim that they cannot learn. You claim their minds are such poor soil that education would be lost on them. Yet they come originally from a climate where nature has given great riches to everything. Should we think that men from there alone were left unfinished and incapable of enjoying the treasures nature has poured out for them? Such a claim is absurd!

Why do you use those instruments of torture? Should one rational being use them on another? Aren't you ashamed to see people of the same nature as you brought so low? And aren't there great dangers for you in treating others this way? Aren't you always afraid of revolt by them? But by changing your conduct and treating your slaves as men, every cause of fear would be banished. They would be faithful, intelligent, and vigorous; and peace, prosperity, and happiness would be yours.

Possible Questions to Raise

- Imagine that you own slaves. What would convince you that it was wrong?
- Which writer could best convince a slave owner that owning slaves is wrong: a slave, a slaveholder, a former slave, or a former slaveholder? Someone else?
- Why do you think Equiano chose the approach he did?

The Centrality of the Text

In Lesson 15, the students consider the third component of writing—the text itself. In the previous four classes, the text came into consideration only as a pure medium between writer and reader. It will now be viewed as a specific tool with definite characteristics, limitations, and possibilities. A text is written at a specific time in particular language and read at a different time. The differences in time and language and the absence of the author raise issues and possibilities to be explored. The students will investigate when they would prefer a text to its author and when the presence of the author would be preferable. The text by Chung Yung, "The Doctrine of the Middle Way," offers us a device for this because although it takes the attitude of a textbook, it is not about a definite subject matter but about life itself.

Interacting with a text is obviously very different from interacting with the writer of the text. In Worksheet 15, students are introduced to that difference by deciding when they would rather have the author present. To examine the interaction of the reader and the text, the students will use a text that is both similar to and different from a type of text they are very familiar with—textbooks. The textbook is neither argumentative nor exploratory. Although a textbook may employ arguments, proofs, or include the invitation to explore, its form is essentially that of providing information. It concerns a definite subject matter that is not open to question. The writer of a textbook knows the subject matter, and the reader needs to learn it. The absence of the author is also appropriate because the author is not offering his thoughts or opinions, but is simply presenting a subject matter. Unlike a poem, for example, the subject matter is distinctly separate from the writer, containing its own language and history. This separation makes the textbook a unique opportunity to examine the interaction between the reader and the text. The textbook structure that is used to frame what is generally considered to be a very personal subject, will help students scrutinize the textbook form and its limitations.

The text is concerned with establishing and dealing with one's own limits and boundaries. *The Doctrine of the Middle Way* gives advice about how to act, how to deal with others, and how to respond to one's station in life. The author does not present a personal account of his own experiences, nor does he present an argument. The reader either accepts or rejects it. Chung Yung is attempting to convey that one becomes a true and real person by working within boundaries and limitations. This is a surprising idea for many of us since we are often told that our aim should be to push beyond our own boundaries and limitations. It is therefore a useful text in scrutinizing texts in general because it gives advice about issues that would result in changing some of our most basic presuppositions.

The three areas in which Chung Yung presents our boundaries are our actions, our relationships to other people, and our station in life. Each of these presents useful avenues for discussion in which the students can compare Chung Yung's statements with their own presuppositions and beliefs. In addition, the Touchstones classes themselves can be usefully contrasted with Chung Yung. In the case of actions, Chung Yung recommends taking action only after complete preparation, whereas Touchstones Discussions place an emphasis on spontaneity. In regard to relationships, Chung Yung contends that friendship and trust come from everyone acting according to duty, whereas your students will have many different ideas about where friendship and trust come from. Chung Yung's final area, acting according to one's station in life, is antithetical to many western beliefs. All of these topics present fruitful avenues for discussion.

During the discussion, observers will be used to help examine the relationship between the reader and the text. The observers should be given the explicit instruction of deciding whether the group has adequately dealt with the text. Useful questions for them to answer are 1) When speakers agreed or disagreed with the text, did they really understand it? 2) Did the group make the effort to understand the text? 3) Did people find or look for examples in the text to support claims they made about it? 4) How could the group have gotten more out of the text?

Lesson Plan 15

1. TEXT..3 minutes
   - Read the text aloud and have students write an opening question.

2. CHOOSE OBSERVERS/PARTICIPANTS...4 minutes
   - Depending upon your class size, choose three to six students to be observers for this discussion.
   - Ask the students who will not be observers to write an opening question they would like the class to discuss. While they are doing this, meet with the group of observers. Instruct them that their task is to determine how effectively the discussion participants deal with the text. Issues they should keep in mind are
       a) When the speakers agreed or disagreed with the text, did they understand what the text claimed?
       b) Did they make an effort to understand it?
       c) How might they have discussed it more adequately?

3. DISCUSSION..18 minutes
   - Have observers sit outside the discussion circle.
   - Have all of the students read their opening questions aloud before you randomly select a student to start the discussion.

4. INDIVIDUAL WORK...2 minutes
   - Ask participants and observers to write a few sentences on whether the discussion dealt adequately with the text and gave the author a fair hearing.

5. DISCUSSION ANALYSIS...10 minutes
   - Have observers report their notes on the discussion. After, allow participants to respond.

6. REVIEW WORKSHEET..6 minutes
   - Have students volunteer their responses for questions 2 and 3. Let this lead to a discussion about when they would prefer a text and when they would prefer a person to convince them.

7. WORKSHEET..2 minutes
   - Distribute Worksheet and Writing Assignment 16.

Total: 45 minutes

Worksheet 15

1. Authors write many different kinds of texts. Depending upon the type and purpose of their writing, you might prefer to have the author present instead of just the text, so you could ask questions, share ideas, debate opinions, or argue your own point of view. In the following list, write "T" where you would prefer just the text and "A" where you would prefer to have the author present. You cannot have both.

_____ a poem

_____ a novel

_____ a diary

_____ a science textbook

_____ a sports article

_____ a recipe

2. Choose one of the items above for which you answered "T", and explain why.

3. Choose one of the items above for which you answered "A", and explain why.

Writing Assignment 15

If someone wanted to change your mind about something you believed very strongly, would you prefer that person do it by speaking to you or writing to you? In your notebook, describe one of your beliefs, and explain the reasons you would prefer a person to persuade you in either speech or writing.

The Doctrine of the Middle Way
Chung Yung

In all business dealings, success comes to those who prepare beforehand. Without this preparation, there will be failure. And when you are going to speak, you must decide beforehand what you are going to say. Then when the time comes, you won't slip up or stutter. And if before setting out on anything, you decide what you plan to do, you will not fall into confusion. Decide beforehand how you will act and there will be no regrets.

Unless those who lead society have gained the confidence of those in the lower ranks, they will never get the support of the mass of the people. But there can be no confidence in leaders unless people who are friends can trust one another. And friends cannot trust one another unless they, in turn, do their duty to their own parents. And there is only one way that enables someone to do his duty. If a person is not true, he cannot do his duty to his parents. But there is only one way for a man to have a real and true self. He must understand what is good, for if he doesn't, he cannot be real and true in himself.

The acts of a true man agree with his position and station in life. If he is a man of wealth, he acts as such. If he is poor, he acts accordingly. A man of wealth does not despise those who are poor. A poor man does not cling to those who are wealthy. Instead, he acts rightly and seeks no favors. If one acts accordingly to one's station, one will feel no resentment of others, nor will others resent him. One will have an easy mind ready and be prepared for whatever happens; unlike a man who is not true and keeps hoping for good luck. This is similar to target-shooting. When a man who is true misses the target, he looks for the cause in himself.

Possible Questions to Raise

- If Chung Yung's advice were written in another manner, would it be more or less convincing? (i.e. if it were a persuasive letter rather than a set of direct instructions.)
- What does Chung Yung mean when he states, "the acts of a true man agree with his position and station in life"?

Exploratory Writing

In Lesson 16, the students will explore whether a fundamental belief can be changed by a counter argument. The text by George Berkeley from *A Treatise Concerning the Principles of Human Knowledge* attacks a belief we all share—that is, that the ideas in our minds are similar to or represent things or objects in the world. Berkeley presents powerful reasons against this belief and yet it is unlikely that anyone has ever been convinced by his arguments. The text and the worksheet encourage students to consider what beliefs might be changed by argument, and whether certain beliefs or attitudes can only be changed by other means, if at all.

Lessons 16 through 21 will move from the persuasive writing of Lessons 11 through 15 into exploratory writing. Exploratory writing occurs when a person investigates his or her most fundamental beliefs—beliefs that are often invisible and implicit. In order to make them explicit, students will examine a case where one of these implicit beliefs is questioned.

We are all familiar with proofs and arguments. We have all tried to prove things to other people, and they have tried to prove things to us. Most of us argue about politics, sports, religion, or current events. We argue with friends, lovers, family, and enemies. Early Touchstones classes were probably filled with arguments and attempted proofs. Proofs and arguments are appealing to us because they respond to our desire for certainty and security. We feel most comfortable and rational when we can give reasons for what we believe. But we all act according to beliefs that cannot be easily supported with proof. Some beliefs are quite complex and have taken years of trial and error to develop. Others seem so natural that it is hard to imagine a time when we did not believe them, such as the belief that one should not touch a hot stove.

However, there is a group of beliefs that seems even more integral to who we are as human beings. These beliefs strangely appear to have always been with us, although, of course, that is highly unlikely. They are the beliefs that make us who and what we are. We might call these beliefs "basic" or "fundamental." Because they go without saying, we hardly notice them. To make such beliefs visible requires a special effort or special circumstances. We often become puzzled when we realize that another person might consider what seems to be an obvious truth to be merely one of our beliefs or opinions. The question the students will confront in today's class is how to become aware of such beliefs and consider changing them. In particular, can someone persuade us or argue us out of them?

The Berkeley text helps the students focus on the issue of unquestioned beliefs by showing how difficult it is to notice, explore, and argue about a belief of this type. The belief Berkeley considers concerns our ideas and their sources. One of our most common experiences is seeing, feeling, or hearing something. For example, imagine you are hungry. You see food on the table, and go to eat it. Generally, we find the food exactly where we saw it, and the feeling of hunger vanishes because we ate. If we articulate a belief that captures this relationship between the food, your sense of sight, your hunger, and the satisfaction of that hunger, it might go something like this: seeing the food, which happens inside of your mind, leads you to eat the food, which is outside you. Another way to describe this occurrence: the seeing, which occurs in our minds, connects us with what we see in the world. The belief that what your senses present to you is actually outside of you appears to be a fundamental belief underlying all human actions. It is not specific to a certain culture, time, place, gender, or sort of upbringing. In fact it is very difficult to consider it a belief at all; rather we take this belief to be an obvious truth. Yet, this is roughly what Berkeley denies. He argues that what is in the mind has no connection or relationship with what is outside the mind.

Berkeley's argument is very complex but the major point is simple. Our knowledge of the outside world comes entirely through our experience—our ideas or sensations. So, we should ask ourselves how do we know there are things in the world that cause our experiences. We assume that objects in the world cause us to experience them but since we only have the experiences we may be merely imagining this. We might be tempted to think that we could somehow step out of our experiences and compare the experiences with objects in the world. But that is illusory since that comparison is simply another experience.

Berkeley's strange argument has a certain power. It is very difficult to dismiss and even harder to accept. Modern versions of this concept, like the movie The Matrix, continue to capture the imagination. Students should discuss the first paragraph of the text, and consider whether there are any obvious flaws in it. However, the main role this text can play for us is quite different. If it is flawed, it is not defective in any simple way. It appears to be an argument one should be able to take seriously. Yet, people continue to behave, speak, and think as if it is patently false. This raises to the surface the main issue: Why a proof or argument against a basic or fundamental belief exerts so little influence, and what, if anything could make us seriously consider changing one of these beliefs? Addressing what effects an argument like this has on us, and why it will not persuade us will be key to the students' exploration of these beliefs.

Lesson Plan 16

1. SMALL GROUP WORK...10 minutes
   - Divide the class into groups of five. They have two assignments: 1) decide whether they would take seriously the argument that 1 + 1 = 3 and explain why or why not, and 2) decide on two truths or beliefs that they would hold onto regardless of any argument made against them.

2. TEXT..3 minutes
   - Read the text aloud and have students write opening questions.

3. INDIVIDUAL WORK...5 minutes
   - Students are to write down the belief they think Berkeley is arguing against.

4. DISCUSSION...25 minutes
   - Randomly select a student to ask the opening question.
   - Note: Later in the discussion, ask if Berkeley's argument persuaded them. Move to a discussion on which types of beliefs can and cannot be changed by argument alone. Solicit examples of inarguable beliefs from the Small Group Work.

5. DISTRIBUTE WRITING ASSIGNMENTS..2 minutes
   - Distribute Worksheet and Writing Assignment 17

Total: 45 minutes

Worksheet 16

1. Imagine someone does not believe any of the claims listed below. Suppose you wished to convince that person by an argument or proof that these claims are true. Rank the claims from 1 to 8 (1 is the hardest to prove and 8 is the easiest to prove).

   a) _____ A certain food tastes good.

   b) _____ It rained yesterday.

   c) _____ Stones fall when they are dropped.

   d) _____ $1 + 1 = 2$

   e) _____ You can run faster than someone else.

   f) _____ A certain rap group is the best.

   g) _____ If a tree fell in a forest and no one heard it, there would still be sound.

   h) _____ Certainty is better than uncertainty.

2. For each of the items in question 1, write down briefly what you consider the best means of convincing someone. For example, for item (a) you might have the person actually taste the food instead of trying to present an argument.

   a)

   b)

   c)

   d)

   e)

   f)

   g)

   h)

Writing Assignment 16

Imagine that someone presents an argument to you that 1+1=3, and you can't refute it. How would you feel if that happened? Would you believe the argument, and change your mind? Would you continue trying to find the flaw in the argument? Or would you decide the argument must be wrong even though you can't find anything wrong with the logic of it? Describe in your notebook how you would deal with this situation and give some reasons for your action.

A Treatise Concerning the Principles of Human Knowledge
George Berkeley

Some truths are so clear to the mind that a man need only open his eyes to see them. One of these is the following: none of the things that we think fill the world exist at all outside of a mind. In other words, things exist only when they are sensed or known by a mind. Whenever they are not sensed or known by me, or are not sensed or known by the mind of any other created spirit, they either do not exist at all or exist in the mind of a spirit which is eternal. It is completely absurd to imagine that an object exists independently of a mind. To convince yourself of this, try to separate in your own thoughts the existence of an object we see from our seeing it.

But you say that although what I sense and know—my own ideas—do not exist outside of a mind, there are things outside of the mind of which my sensations and thoughts are copies. I answer, a sensation or thought can be like nothing else but a sensation or thought. A color or shape, both of which I see, can be like nothing else but a color or shape. If we look into our thoughts, we will realize that it is impossible to think of any likeness except between our ideas. Again, I ask if these external things, of which our ideas are supposed to be copies, can be sensed. If so, I have gained my point. If they can't be sensed, then how can a color I see be like what is invisible? How can a hardness I feel be like that which cannot be touched?

Some people distinguish between what they call primary and secondary qualities. By primary qualities, they mean the size or shape of a body, its motion, rest, and the fact that it is solid. By secondary, they mean colors, sounds, tastes, smells, and so forth. These people claim that these latter qualities exist only in our minds. But the primary qualities are said to be copies or images of things outside the mind. Size, shape, rest, and motion are thought to exist in something they call matter. By matter, we are to understand an object that can neither sense nor think anything, and in which size, shape, and motion really exist. But are not size, shape and motion also ideas existing in the mind? And, as we agreed, an idea can be like nothing but another idea. Therefore, these qualities cannot exist in an object that can neither sense nor think. But this is what matter is supposed to be. Therefore, what is called matter is absurd.

Possible Questions to Raise

- How do we know things are real?
- Does Berkeley's argument make you unsure of whether the things around you are real? Why or why not?
- If Berkeley were in this room, how would you respond to this argument?
- Can anyone summarize the difference between what Berkeley calls primary and secondary qualities of things?

Discussions and Fundamental Beliefs

In the last lesson, the students considered whether arguments and proofs could make us modify or change fundamental beliefs. Since such beliefs often act as the premises for our proofs and arguments, it is generally unlikely that we can modify them by those tools alone. And as we saw in the last lesson, such proofs often don't change our beliefs at all. The next issue to consider is whether fundamental beliefs can be discussed. Can we utilize discussion as a format in which such beliefs are made explicit, investigated, modified, or perhaps even rejected?

Discussions are often successful when the group attempts to reach a decision or conclusion even though all of the participants are equally uncertain about the result. The effort to reach a single result keeps the group focused, while the common uncertainty allows the members of the group to take risks, to initiate suggestions, and to explore possibilities. When uncertainty is acceptable and no one pretends to have the right answer or has a passionate stake in the result, discussions can and do occur. Yet these circumstances are fairly rare, since in everyday life people usually do have a stake in one result rather than other. Group decisions can have consequences that threaten beliefs or opinions about which the individuals are not willing to allow uncertainty. Discussions concerning fundamental beliefs are of this type—people feel so certain of their beliefs that they often cannot allow uncertainty, even if it is merely for the sake of discussion.

In Lesson 17, the students will consider whether fundamental beliefs can be discussed or whether agreement about such beliefs is necessary to allow discussion of other, less primary, beliefs. They will investigate what is necessary for a discussion to succeed. The text for this lesson is a sermon by the Buddha, *On Being Abused by Others*. In the sermon, two men confront one another rather than attempt a discussion. By considering this situation and Worksheet 17, the students will spell out when and if certain discussions are possible.

Our basic beliefs are the ones we all share and take to be undeniable truths. They are the ones that make us the kinds of beings that we are. The students will therefore have to not be themselves in order to discuss such beliefs. The result is a kind of confusion. How do we pretend to be uncertain about something we believe with absolute certainty? And, if we can pretend to be uncertain of a basic belief, how do we discuss it? Our beliefs are so interconnected that to doubt one of them will mean we must also doubt others. Once the uncertainty spreads, it becomes unclear what common ground we can find, if any, on which to base the discussion itself.

The Buddha text is useful for raising these concerns because the two men in the story confront an issue that should be discussable—whether a person should respond to evil with goodness. The story is an account of a meeting between the Buddha and an unnamed man. The Buddha has observed how much misery people can cause one another. He believes that people are cruel to one another in order to satisfy their own vanity and pride. A man who heard about the Buddha's belief comes to him. Instead of speaking to the Buddha, the stranger hits and curses him. It is not clear from the text why the man is violent. Some possibilities might be that he comes to test the Buddha because he doesn't believe someone can really act according to this principle. Another possibility is that the Buddha's belief so angers the man that he acts in this way out of passion.

The Buddha's response is entirely in speech—he neither strikes nor hugs the man who has struck and cursed him. Rather he asks him a question about a general issue—giving presents and refusing to accept them. The man gives the obvious answer—if you offer someone a present and the other refuses it, it still belongs to you. This is the last we hear from the man. From this point on, the Buddha argues that because he does not accept the evil from the man, the man causes evil to himself. His unaccepted evil act will cause him misery and pain. The Buddha has very definite ideas about evil, misery, and pain; and according to the Buddha, it is possible for people to accept or reject the evil done to them.

Lesson Plan 17

1. SMALL GROUP WORK...8 minutes
   - Divide the class into groups of students who had the same answer for question 2 on Worksheet 17.
   - Have groups explain their choice, providing reasons or examples.

2. GROUP REPORTS...10 minutes
   - In the large group, ask each group to report and have others respond to each group's reasons.

3. TEXT..4 minutes
   - Read the text aloud and have the students write an opening question.

4. DISCUSSION..21 minutes
   - Note: Later in the discussion, have the students consider whether or not they feel repaying evil with good is an issue that can be discussed. Relate this to the issues brought up by the small groups.

5. DISTRIBUTE WRITING ASSIGNMENTS...2 minutes
   - Distribute Writing Assignment and Worksheet 18

Total: 45 minutes

Worksheet 17

1. Which subjects would most likely lead to a useless argument instead of a cooperative discussion? Rank the following topics from 1 to 4 (1 is the least likely to lead to argument and 4 is the most likely).

   _____ a) Whether abortion should be legal.

   _____ b) Whether God exists.

   _____ c) Whether men are superior to women.

   _____ d) Whether a person should repay evil with good.

2. Which of the following reasons best explains why these kinds of discussions are difficult? Add an additional reason of your own.

   _____ a) People don't know enough about the subject.

   _____ b) People feel too strongly about the subject.

   _____ c) People won't say what they really believe.

   _____ d) People won't listen to others who disagree.

   _____ e) People have nothing in common on which to base the discussion.

   _____ f) _____

Writing Assignment 17

Decide whether you agree or disagree with the following statement, and write a paragraph in your notebook defending that stance.

"If someone does something bad to you, you should respond by doing something good."

On Being Abused by Others
Buddha

And the Buddha, the Blessed One, looked at the way human beings treat one another. He saw how much misery comes from foolish acts that are only done to gratify vanity and pride. And the Buddha said: "If someone does wrong to me, I will return to him the protection of my love; the more evil comes from him, the more good shall go from me."

A man who had learned that the Buddha believed in the principle of great love, which commands us to return good to anyone who does evil to us, came and cursed at him and struck him. The Buddha was silent.

When the man had finished abusing him, the Buddha asked him, "Son, if a man refuses to accept a present that is given to him, to whom would it belong?" The man replied, "It would belong to the person who offered it."

"My son," said the Buddha. "You have cursed me and struck me, but I refuse to accept it. You must keep it for yourself. It will become a source of great misery and pain to you. As the echo belongs to the sounds that made it, and the shadow to the object creating the shadow, so misery belongs to the person who makes it." The man did not reply, and the Buddha continued. "A wicked man who tries to harm a good man is like a person who looks up and spits at heaven. The spit doesn't reach heaven, but falls back on the spitter."

Possible Questions to Raise

- Why do you think the man reacts so violently to the Buddha's views?
- Is it likely the Buddha convinced the man of his principle of repaying evil with good?
- On what underlying beliefs might the Buddha's views be based?
- Does your own experience with evil acts confirm or counter the Buddha's views?
- What else might he have done or said to convince the man?

18

Why These Texts?

Touchstones Discussions consist of three components—a discussion process, the experiences and thoughts of the members of the group, and selected non-contemporary texts. In Lesson 17, the students tried to articulate the reasons some discussions are successful and others fail. The criteria concerned issues of expertise, a willingness to share thoughts, a desire or perceived need to listen, and particularly the kind of agreement necessary among the participants.

Touchstones Discussions are not discussions among friends, but discussion that involve people who represent the entire spectrum of feelings, affections, goals, backgrounds, and beliefs. One of the roles of the text in a Touchstones Discussion is to supply the common ground that is a prerequisite for discussions among friends. To fulfill this function, however, requires special texts. First, the texts cannot reinforce the opinions of some participants and run counter to those of others, as a volatile newspaper article on a current event might. All of the participants must have roughly the same degree of agreement with the text, although this agreement need not be concerning the same details. Second, the texts must not convey the impression that specialized knowledge is required to consider the issues raised—they cannot use language or refer to concepts that require an expert's translation. Third, while the texts deal with recognizable issues, they must do so in unfamiliar ways—it must simultaneously present itself as a focus of familiar common concern and be an object of some puzzlement to all members of the group. This third characteristic has been described throughout Touchstones' materials as the blending of the familiar and unfamiliar in texts. All of these elements are satisfied by the use of non-contemporary classics of the western and non-western worlds.

These very same characteristics of texts that make possible the development of discussion skills also allow the discussion to bring to the surface our most fundamental beliefs. The texts that society considers to be "classic" explicitly contain the unspoken presuppositions of our culture, and the beliefs on which we operate without question or examination. Modern fundamental beliefs become visible within these classics because they connect the very same fundamental beliefs with opinions, concerns, and attitudes that appear old-fashioned, silly, alien, or strange. The interconnection and union in a text of radically different kinds of beliefs can make our most fundamental presuppositions explicit for the first time. In this lesson, the students will explore how this works in a Touchstones text.

In Lesson 17, discussions of issues rather than texts were considered. In Lesson 18, the students will explore how texts affect what can be discussed and the nature of discussions. In particular, they will investigate the role of the Touchstones texts themselves. The text for this lesson, Benjamin Banneker's *Plan for a Department of Peace for the United States*, is a good example of how the familiar and unfamiliar are blended in a Touchstones text. It will help the students begin to notice this dimension of the texts they have been discussing in Touchstones. Banneker's text is a proposal for a governmental institution—a Department of Peace. The text has a deep level of familiarity, because it concerns our own government and the constitution under which we still live. The topics it brings forward are also familiar. He discusses education, religion, the military, and capital punishment. Though each concern is recognizable, a deep unfamiliarity is also present, since Banneker's proposal was never accepted. Who ever heard of a Department of Peace? No nation has such a government department, although most have a War Department or a Department of Defense. The text therefore recounts a possible world that could have been ours, but is not.

The students will directly examine the features of this Touchstones text in their individual and small group work. They will begin with a discussion of the text and then move onto small group work, in which they will explore the familiar and unfamiliar characteristics of Banneker's text and try to determine the central issue of it.

Lesson Plan 18

1. TEXT...4 minutes
   - Read the text aloud and have the students write opening questions.

2. DISCUSSION...8 minutes
   - Have the students vote on whether they would choose to include a Department of Peace in the United States Constitution. Ask for reasons for and against the proposal.
   - Randomly select a student to ask the opening question.

3. SMALL GROUP WORK...8 minutes
   - Divide the students into groups of four or five.
   - Have the students describe what is familiar and what is unfamiliar to them about the text.
   - Have them decide what issue from the text best describes what they talked about in the discussion.

4. GROUP REPORTS...10 minutes
   - In the large circle, have each group report the issue they chose and explain why. Encourage others to respond to each report.

5. DISCUSSION...13 minutes
   - Ask the class what role the text played in this discussion.
   - Explore other possible texts that could have been used to deal with the same issue by asking how different texts would have affected the discussion.

6. DISTRIBUTE WRITING ASSIGNMENTS..2 minutes
   - Distribute Text, Writing Assignment, and Worksheet 19
   - Note: The students are to prepare the text for the next class ahead of time and will need to take their books home with them.

Total: 45 minutes

Worksheet 18

1. If you were going to lead a cooperative discussion about the issues listed below, would it be better to have the discussion with or without a text? For each below, mark your choice.

	With text	Without
a) Is right to get even with someone?	_____	_____
b) Is right to experiment on animals?	_____	_____
c) Is it desirable to live forever?	_____	_____
d) Why are some people afraid of math and science?	_____	_____
e) Is abortion right?	_____	_____

2. Choose one of the issues for which you thought a text was necessary, and explain why.

Writing Assignment 18

For the same issue you used in question 2, what sort of text would be most useful? Choose one of the answers below and then write a paragraph in your notebook persuading someone to use the type of text you selected.

a) A recent newspaper magazine article defending one of the positions.
b) A text describing both sides of the issue.
c) A story that illustrates the issue.
d) A text that presents the issue or concern in a very unfamiliar way.

A Plan for a Department of Peace for the United States
Benjamin Banneker

Many defects have been pointed out in the new federal constitution by its enemies. However, no one has noticed its total silence about an office that would be of greatest importance to the welfare of the United States—an office for promoting and preserving everlasting peace in our country. It is hoped that no one will object to establishing such an office, now, while we are at war with the Indians. The War Office itself was established during a time of peace, so it is reasonable that a Peace Office be established in time of war.

The plan of this office is as follows:

1. Let there be a Secretary of Peace who will be a believer in the principles of our republic and a sincere Christian; for the principles of our government and of Christianity are no less friendly to universal or everlasting peace than they are to universal and equal liberty.

2. Let this Secretary be given the power to establish and maintain free schools in every city, village, and township. Let him be made responsible for the talents, principles and morals of all the teachers. Let the youth of this country be taught reading, writing, and arithmetic and the doctrines of a religion of some kind. The Christian religion might be preferred to others because this religion teaches us not only to cultivate peace with all men, but to forgive, and even to love our very enemies. Christianity also teaches us that God alone can take a human life, and that we rebel against his laws whenever we execute and kill any of his creatures in any way.

3. In order to encourage respect for human life and a horror at the shedding of human blood, let all those laws be repealed that allow juries, judges, sheriffs, and executioners to kill a prisoner in cold blood in any criminal case whatever. Until we change our laws in this way and eliminate capital punishment, it will be impossible to introduce universal and perpetual peace into our country.

4. To subdue that desire for war that education, added to human weakness, has produced, a familiarity with the weapons and tools of death as well as military shows should be carefully avoided. Military uniforms and titles should be forbidden. Military parades should not be permitted. They lessen the horrors of battle by connecting these horrors with the charms of order and the excitement of marching bands. There should be no military uniforms. Military uniforms fascinate the minds of young men and lead them away from serious and useful professions. If there were no uniforms, there would probably be no armies. Lastly, military ranks feed vanity and pride. They should be discontinued in our country because they encourage ideas in the mind that lessen a sense of the foolishness and miseries of war.

Possible Questions to Raise

- What parts of Banneker's argument do you find most persuasive?
- What might be different in our society if his proposal had been accepted?
- What would society's reaction be like if this proposal were made today?
- What kinds of arguments do you imagine people made against this proposal?

Exploratory Writing and Cooperative Thinking

In order to view fundamental beliefs as mere beliefs, students will practice writing an argument in favor of a belief with which they disagree. This technique enables the students temporarily to consider deeply held convictions to be uncertain—an exercise that prepares the way for understanding how very different beliefs can arise among people.

During the discussion, the focus will be on cooperative thinking. In past discussions, the students worked together by pooling their experiences, by sharing what they know, by sometimes building on what one another offer, by listening to other perspectives, and by acknowledging that different students have differing strengths. They found that they could teach and learn from one another and so they have worked and learned cooperatively. The next step is not only to work and learn cooperatively but to think cooperatively.

Cooperative thinking occurs through discussions and is the sequel to the activity we have called exploratory writing. In typical forms of writing, we present what we know, believe, think, or want. In exploratory writing, rather than presenting claims of which we are certain, we temporarily view our certainties as uncertainties in order to explore them. Having done this, we need others to actively explore them.

Normally, we regard thinking as a solitary activity. But each of us is too close to ourselves to effectively examine our own beliefs. If we were to try, we would generally end up simply reaffirming our beliefs, dismissing the alternatives, or remaining unaware of the possible alternatives. Lesson 19 will guide students toward thinking cooperatively by using a text with which most people will both agree and disagree, and by drawing out the similarities and differences within the group. This will be the students' first introduction to the cooperative thinking that will be the focus of the last section of this volume.

The discussion will focus on practicing cooperative thinking to explore and investigate fundamental beliefs. The group will investigate the inter connection among fundamental beliefs. Just as the students required the Touchstones text to achieve distance from shared beliefs, they now require the diversity among them—their distance from one another—to bring out how that belief is connected with other beliefs. They will use Emerson's text to imagine how Emerson would view and participate in a Touchstones Discussion and compare that with their own perceptions of their shared experience. For the first time, the students will read and prepare the text before coming to class.

In the last class, the discussion process and Touchstones texts were explicitly utilized to isolate and highlight some beliefs we can consider fundamental. However, exploring such a belief requires another step that will be introduced in this class—exploratory writing. Noticing a fundamental belief has already required a strategy. Fundamental beliefs only become visible when either they or their consequences are set in contrast to beliefs we do not hold. This should not be surprising since it is the hallmark of fundamental beliefs that they are so ever-present that we don't even notice them.

Before today's class, using the opinions from Emerson's text *On Self-Reliance* the students will practice exploratory writing concerning a text that has a relatively high degree of familiarity. On the worksheet, the students will be asked to order a list of beliefs, each of which is proposed by Emerson in the text, based upon their degree of agreement with each believe. The writing assignment asks the students to compose an argument in favor of the belief with which they agree the least.

Emerson's text argues that we should focus on ourselves and not on others. He is very critical of envy and imitation because they turn our focus away from ourselves. For Emerson, each individual is unique and that uniqueness means that we all notice things that others do not. When we imitate someone, we try to take on his or her perspective rather than become aware of our own. In this sense, Emerson's argument can be considered to be opposed to the work of Touchstones. This difference will be the foundation for cooperative thinking in this lesson.

The discussion will not focus on actual beliefs. Rather, students will cooperatively attempt to imagine Emerson's views toward discussions, how he would participate, and how his participation would differ from that of the students. By doing this, they will be setting their own beliefs aside and imagining those of others. In addition, the students should discuss whether the discussion process helps individuals achieve the goals for which Emerson argues.

Lesson Plan 19

1. REVIEW WORKSHEET...10 minutes
   - Have the students show, by raising their hands, which of the seven opinions they agree with most and which they agree with least. Put the results on the board.
   - Compare the results with students' answers to questions 2 and 3.
   - Have the students explain their answers to questions 2 and 3, and allow a discussion of how they decided on their answers.
   - Note: You may also ask if any students answered questions 2 and 3 with opinions that they did not rank as highest or lowest and have them explain why.

2. TEXT...2 minutes
   - Even though the students have read the text before the class, read it aloud once more, and have students form opening questions.

3. SMALL GROUP WORK...12 minutes
   - Divide the class into groups of three.
   - Have the groups compare answers to question 4 and decide how Emerson would participate in discussions for each behavior on the list.
   - Have the groups find a passage in the text that supports their choice.
   - Note: They are instructed to find a passage for every item on the list, but it is not necessary that every group finish within the allotted time.

4. DISCUSSION...19 minutes
   - Randomly select a student to ask the opening question.

5. DISTRIBUTE WRITING ASSIGNMENTS...2 minutes
   - Distribute Writing Assignment and Worksheet 20

Total: 45 minutes

Worksheet 19

1. Before reading Emerson's argument, rank the opinions listed below on a scale from 1 to 7 (1 is the opinion with which you most agree, and 7 is the opinion with which you least agree).

   _____ Imitating other people is a kind of suicide.

   _____ The power that lives in each of us is new in nature and only we know what we can do.

   _____ Usually we only half express ourselves.

   _____ The divine idea in each of us can be trusted as long as we are faithful to it.

   _____ Trust yourself.

   _____ Accept the place that God has found for you and the friends you have.

   _____ We are guides and benefactors of others, obeying God, and fighting against darkness and evil.

2. Which of the above opinions do you think the largest number of your classmates would agree with most? In other words, which opinion will most students have ranked with a 1.

3. Which of the above opinions do you think the largest number of your classmates would agree with least?

4. Read the Emerson text, "On Self-Reliance." Then do the following exercise:

Listed below are some ways people behave in discussions. If Emerson were a member of your Touchstones group, what do you think he would be like in the discussion? Put a check in the "Emerson" column next to the items that you think would describe Emerson's behavior. Then put a check in the "You" column next to the items that describe your participation in the discussions.

	Emerson	You
Tries to be understood by everyone.	❏	❏
Says interesting things.	❏	❏
Brings up personal experiences and allows them to be discussed.	❏	❏
Helps the group understand the text.	❏	❏
Argues well and convinces others.	❏	❏
Builds on what others say.	❏	❏
Asks important questions.	❏	❏
Admits being wrong.	❏	❏

5. What do you think would be the major difference between the way you participate and the way Emerson would?

Writing Assignment 19

In your notebook, write a short argument in favor of the item in question 1 that you ranked a 7—the one you agreed with least

On Self-Reliance
Ralph Waldo Emerson

There comes a time in every man's education when he comes to the conclusion that envying other people is a kind of ignorance, and that imitating other people is a kind of suicide. He discovers that he must take himself as he is, for better or worse. He discovers that, though the universe is full of good things, none of them can nourish him. He is nourished only through his own labor or through the gifts nature has given to him.

The power that lives in every person is new in nature, and no one except he knows what he can do. Even he doesn't know until he has tried. It isn't for nothing that a certain face or a certain fact makes an impression on him and on no one else. His eye has viewed that scene so that that particular person's face and that particular fact might be seen and revealed through him to others.

Usually we only half express ourselves. It is as if we were ashamed of the divine idea that each of us represents. This divine idea in each of us can be trusted as long as we are faithful to it. But God does not want his work done by cowards. A man is happy and relieved when he has put his heart into his work and done his best. But if he has not, then whatever he has said or done will give him no peace. His spirit and inspiration will desert him; he will invent nothing; and he will lose hope.

Trust yourself! Every heart is tuned to that string. Accept the place that God has found for you, and the friends you have. Great men have always done so, and have trusted, like children, in the circumstances of their lives. They showed that what could most be counted on was already in their hearts, and would come out in the work of their minds and hands. We are now these men and must accept the same destiny. We are neither children nor sick people living in a protected corner. We are not cowards trying to escape a revolution. We are guides and benefactors, obeying God, and fighting against darkness and evil.

Possible Questions to Raise

- Do you think Emerson would recommend Touchstones to students? Why or why not?
- Can discussions help achieve the goals he outlines in the text?
- What do you think Emerson means when he says "usually we only half express ourselves?"

Forming New Beliefs

When a fundamental belief changes, often it appears that we ourselves change. The change is similar to what someone might experience when falling in love. When we fall in love, often the whole world, ourselves included, takes on a different shape and color. Though this specifically involves our relation to a single person, the change spreads through other profound dimensions of our experience.

A change in a fundamental belief is similar but goes even deeper. For example, most of us believe that peace is preferable to war. Were we to believe that war is preferable to peace, we would not be merely exchanging one opinion for another, we would be changing our sense of what being alive means, the nature of family, security and prosperity, and the nature of society and the role of an individual in society. Everything we typically cherish, hope for, and dread would shift. We, ourselves, and the world we inhabit would be different; we would become different people.

Changing such a belief therefore reorganizes an entire network of interrelated beliefs. Once we have changed the belief and adjusted these interrelations, we become different. However, in the process of changing the belief, we are in a kind of no-man's land, an uncharted territory. We have surrendered our certainties and have not yet adopted new ones. While all of this will not happen in a Touchstones Discussion, in Lesson 20, the students will experiment with procedures they may someday need to undertake.

In Touchstones Discussions, the students have been exploring and investigating fundamental beliefs. Probably, they have not and will not change them. However, in this class they will begin to think about what such changes are like. Changing a fundamental belief and forming a new one is different from modifying other beliefs. In forming a new fundamental belief we change who we are, not just something we believe, as when we change an opinion about a fact. Fundamental beliefs define the ideas they contain. Changing the belief changes the ideas. The students will consider such changes in the worksheet and also in Immanuel Kant's text, from *Idea for a Universal History*, which articulates a new relation between conflict and cooperation.

We have all had the experience of changing our opinions. Many things we considered true, we later discovered to be false and vice versa. These are ordinary occurrences. Equally ordinary is the experience of having been uncertain about an opinion and deciding or recognizing that we have become more certain it was true or false at a later date. We change our minds frequently about facts and people, and about our likes and dislikes. However, changes in fundamental beliefs are radically different.

In the worksheet for this lesson the students were asked to create two lists of opposites and consider whether each list has anything in common. The opposing concepts overlap some of the opposing pairs that were mentioned in the Introduction as characterizing a division within technological life, and which form some of the fundamental beliefs of our culture. Among these opposing concepts and attitudes are private/public, trust/distrust, risk/control, and competition/cooperation. The task in Lesson 20 is to consider whether ways could be found to modify or re-conceive both members of such a pair to diminish their opposition. Kant's text can offer us a simple approach because he tries to show that the members of some of these pairs of opposites require one another.

Lesson Plan 20

1. SMALL GROUP WORK..15 minutes
   - Divide the class into groups of four.
   - Have the groups discuss their answers on the worksheet and come to agreement on question 1.
   - Have them help one another provide a reason for their answer to question 2.

2. TEXT...4 minutes
   - Read the text aloud and have the students form opening questions.

3. DISCUSSION..15 minutes
   - Randomly select a student to ask the opening question.
   - Note: Make sure to bring up the claim that morality and civilization arise from conflict and unsociable behavior, if the students do not initiate this line of discussion on their own.

4. DISCUSSION REFLECTION..9 minutes
   - Ask the students how they feel they have changed in Touchstones classes through this year as individuals and as a group. In particular, ask them to consider what they think the group needs to improve on during the rest of the year and what already existing group strengths can be built on to accomplish this goal.

5. DISTRIBUTE WRITING ASSIGNMENT..2 minutes
   - Distribute Writing Assignment and Worksheet 21

Total: 45 minutes

Worksheet 20

1. Match each of the following concepts to its opposite concept. The exercise has been started for you. Before you write the words in the blanks, decide which member of each pair belongs in Column A, and which member of each pair belongs in Column B. Column A should contain all of the concepts that seem to fit in with "War," and Column B should contain all of the concepts that seem to fit in with "Peace." When you are finished, Column A and Column B should each contain concepts that are somewhat similar to one another, and each row should contain a pair of opposites.

Concepts:

Cooperation	Public	~~War~~	Trust
~~Peace~~	Competition	Generosity	Reason
Feelings	Suspicion	Selfishness	Private

Column A		**Column B**
War	is the opposite of	Peace
_____	is the opposite of	_____
_____	is the opposite of	_____
_____	is the opposite of	_____
_____	is the opposite of	_____
_____	is the opposite of	_____

2. Of all of the items you placed in Column A, choose one that best represents what is similar about all the items in that list. In other words, choose one that might make a good heading or title for that list. Then choose one for Column B.

Column A:

Column B:

Writing Assignment 20

Choosing one of the pairs of opposites from the list above, write a paragraph or two describing how the item in Column A could lead to the item in Column B. For example, if you chose the pair we began with, war and peace, you would need to write an argument how the condition of war could lead to the condition of peace.

Idea for a Universal History
Immanuel Kant

In order to bring about the development of all the abilities of human beings, nature makes use of the conflict or hostility of human beings against one another. In the end, this conflict is the cause of the lawful order that exists among human beings. By hostility I mean the tendency of human beings who, even when entering into society, bring along with them an opposition to others that threatens to break up society. This I call the "unsocial sociability" of human beings.

Every person has a tendency to associate with other persons because he feels that in society he is more than merely a single person with very limited powers. But he also has a strong tendency to isolate himself from others. This is because he finds in himself the unsocial characteristic of wanting everything to go according to his wishes. He expects opposition from everyone because he knows that he himself is inclined to oppose others.

This opposition awakens all his powers. It provokes him to conquer his laziness, and it awakens his lust for power and wealth. It makes him want to rise above other human beings whom he cannot tolerate but from whom he cannot separate himself.

This is the first step toward civilization. In this way, all human talents are developed and refined. This is also the beginning of the development of moral principles from man's natural moral feelings. All human beings possess these unsocial characteristics. Our selfishness is a sign of this. Without our conflict with others there would be no development of talents and abilities. Human beings would be good-natured like sheep in a herd. They would not rise above the other animals and achieve rational thought.

Therefore, we should be thankful to nature for our unsociability, our competitiveness, and our desires for wealth and power. Without these things our potentialities would remain forever undeveloped. Human beings desire peace; but nature, which knows better what is good for man, desires war. Men want to live comfortably; nature plunges them into trouble and hardship so that they can find the way out of these things. The same unsociable characteristics, which cause so many bad results, also drive men to greater efforts and to the development of their powers. Perhaps these unsociable characteristics show the wisdom of God, and not the hand of an evil spirit who spoiled God's work out of envy.

Possible Questions to Raise

- Do you agree with Kant when he says, "without our conflict with others there would be no development of talents and abilities?"
- Can you think of a time when something good has come out of acting selfishly?
- Is being selfish always bad?
- Can you think of other "unsociable" qualities, besides the ones listed in the text, that can make humans aspire to achieve things?

Knowing the Past, Shaping the Future

The focus of the third unit of this Guide is having students teach themselves. Students will have to learn how to identify when they can teach themselves and when they need to learn from others. They will have to explore ideas and issues that are new to them as well as familiar issues in unfamiliar ways. The work the students have already done in Touchstones has set the stage for this kind of learning by offering them insights into and awareness of their fundamental beliefs, presuppositions, and other habits that can impede their learning.

The ten texts that complete this volume give the students the opportunity to actively practice teaching themselves and others. The students will have the chance to develop an idea for themselves, compare it to their classmates' ideas, and then to an author's words in order to get a complete picture of their own contributions as well as the potential contributions of other students and the text.

The text from Booker T. Washington offers the class an opportunity to discuss the effect that knowing one's ancestry can have on how one lives his or her life. Washington tells a story from childhood in which his teacher asks his name during the roll call at school. Upon hearing the other students use two names, he realizes that he needs a name in addition to Booker, and gives himself the surname Washington. Later, he learns that his mother had given him the surname Taliaferro, and so he keeps both names and becomes Booker Taliaferro Washington. He then discusses the effects of knowing one's heritage on the way one lives his or her life.

The topic of ancestry, or heritage, and the awareness of one's own heritage, directly relates to the idea of teaching oneself: in both cases, we must examine how external situations and influences affect a person's choices. The text's description of the positive and negative effects of knowing one's heritage is an issue that many of your students may have never considered. You may wish to discuss the difference between the words "ancestry" and "heritage," and remind students that heritage can include not only family, but cultural, religious, and ethnic aspects as well. The worksheet will ask students to explore both sides of knowing one's heritage. Critically examining issues from different perspectives, determining one's own opinion, completing an argument, and constructing arguments for opinions they do not have will all be recurring activities for the rest of the classes. And by comparing their answers to those of their classmates, they will be able to explore the many different approaches one can take.

In the Individual Work, the students will be asked to imagine what they might do if given the chance to rename themselves. In small groups, the students will be told that they are to rename their school and to think about all of the characteristics of the school that would be important to them in choosing a name.

Writing Assignment 21 will ask students to agree or disagree with a quote from the Washington text and to support whatever stance they take. Having practiced exploratory writing in the previous sessions, students now apply critical thinking as they develop an argument and come up with reasons and examples to support their stance.

Lesson Plan 21

1. SMALL GROUP WORK..10 minutes
   - Divide the class into groups of four or five. Groups are to rename the school after a famous person. They should decide upon the name and describe the characteristics of the person that make him or her worthy of having the school named after him or her.

2. GROUP REPORTS...8 minutes
   - Ask groups follow-up questions about how they came to their decisions.

3. TEXT..3 minutes
   - Read the text aloud and have the students read it again silently.

4. OPENING QUESTIONS...3 minutes
   - Have students write opening questions.

5. DISCUSSION...20 minutes
   - Open the discussion using a student's opening question. Later, ask what can be helpful or harmful about knowing one's ancestry or heritage. Other topics can include the benefits of naming oneself.

6. DISTRIBUTE WRITING ASSIGNMENTS..1 minute
   - Distribute Writing Assignment and Worksheet 22

Total: 45 minutes

Worksheet 21

Knowing one's heritage and ancestry can have various consequences on how we live our lives. Below, think of four or five positive and negative effects of knowing your heritage and ancestry.

1. List possible benefits of knowing your heritage.

2. List possible negative effects of knowing your heritage.

3. If you had the chance to rename yourself with any name you wanted, what name would you choose? Why?

Writing Assignment 21

1. The following statement is an excerpt from the reading for Lesson 21. Choose a stance towards the following statement (you can agree with it, disagree with it, or agree with some parts and disagree with others) and write an argument supporting your opinion.

   "The influence of ancestry is important in helping any individual or race move forward as long as not too much reliance is placed upon it."

2. Write an opening question for the discussion on Up From Slavery.

Up from Slavery
Booker T. Washington

From the time when I could remember anything, I had been called simply "Booker." Before going to school it had never occurred to me that it was needful or appropriate to have an additional name. However, when I heard the school-roll called, I noticed that all of the children had at least two names, and some of them indulged in what seemed to me the extravagance of having three. I was confused because I knew that the teacher would demand of me at least two names, and I had only one. By the time the occasion came for declaring my name, an idea occurred to me that I thought would solve this situation.

When the teacher asked me what my full name was, I calmly told him "Booker Washington," as if I had been called by that name all my life; and by that name I have since been known. Later in life I found that my mother had given me the name of "Booker Taliaferro" soon after I was born, but somehow that part of my name seemed to disappear, and for a long while was forgotten. But as soon as I found out about it I revived it, and made my full name "Booker Taliaferro Washington." I think there are not many men in our country who have had the privilege of naming themselves in the way that I have.

More than once I had tried to picture myself in the position of a boy or man with an honored and distinguished ancestry that I could trace back through a period of hundreds of years, and who had not only inherited a name, but also a fortune and a proud family home. And yet, I have sometimes had the feeling that if I had inherited these, and had been a member of a more popular race, I should have been inclined to yield to the temptation of depending upon my ancestry and my color to do that for me which I should do for myself. Years ago I resolved that because I had no ancestry that anyone knew of, I would leave a record of which my children would be proud, and which might encourage them to still greater effort.

The influence of ancestry is important in helping any individual or race move forward as long as not too much reliance is place upon it. The very fact that a boy is conscious that, if he fails in life, he will disgrace the whole family record, extending back through many generations, is of tremendous value in helping him to resist temptations. The fact that the individual has behind him and surrounding him a proud family history and connections serves as a stimulus to help him to overcome obstacles when striving for success.

Possible Questions to Raise

- If you got to rename yourself, what name would you choose? Why?
- What would be the benefit of naming yourself?
- Would knowing your heritage help you? How might it hurt you?
- What does Washington see as the harmful aspects of knowing one's ancestry?
- If you didn't know your ancestry, how might that change you?
- If you found out that one of your ancestors was a great king, how would that affect you?

Learning from Other Perspectives

Students will practice teaching themselves by exploring an issue from an unfamiliar angle: how striving to obtain certain things—money, power, fame, or pleasure— might make them unhappy. They will also assume a perspective other than their own and compare their results with those of their classmates.

As the previous lesson helped students begin teaching themselves by examining both sides of an issue, Lesson 22 offers them the opportunity to explore an argument that is counter to some of their normal thoughts. While there are many examples and arguments about how having a great deal of money or fame may leave someone unhappy, most people strive to attain a certain amount of money and fame. In addition, the arguments that we usually encounter describing the negative effects of fame, for example, are generally focused on the annoyances or inconveniences that it brings with it. In the text, *Consolation of Philosophy*, Boethius describes how the very focus on maintaining wealth, honor, fame, power, and pleasure might bring dissatisfaction. With money, there is the worry over keeping it, and with honor comes a debt to those who honor you.

Students will practice examining another aspect of learning to teach oneself—the question of when we should seek to learn from others. The worksheet asks students to decide which person they would seek to learn about the downside of each of the five things for which people strive. They are then to explain why they chose that person as someone from whom they can learn. Further, Writing Assignment 22 asks them to imagine that they are the person from whom they choose to learn, and to write from that person's perspective.

In small groups, the class will compare their answers about each of the items and come to an agreement about them. As the groups report, be sure to ask them to explain why they chose each of the people they chose and ask other groups to decide if they think each group chose wisely.

Boethius also distinguishes between pleasure and happiness in the text. For Boethius, happiness is not a momentary or temporary thing. Exploring Boethius' idea of happiness during the discussion will be a good way to help students explore what might be a strange idea.

Lesson Plan 22

1. SMALL GROUP WORK...8 minutes
   - Divide the class into groups of four or five. Have the students compare their answers to question 1 from Worksheet 22 and decide upon one answer for each of the items.

2. GROUP REPORTS..10 minutes
   - Ask each group follow-up questions regarding their choice and ask other groups to comment.

3. TEXT...2 minutes
   - Read the text aloud and have students read it again silently.

4. DISCUSSION...24 minutes
   - Randomly choose a student to ask the opening question. Later, move the discussion toward how these same things can make them unhappy.

5. DISTRIBUTE WRITING ASSIGNMENTS..1 minute
   - Distribute Writing Assignment and Worksheet 23   1 minute

Total: 45 minutes

Worksheet 22

1. The following is a list of things people often believe will make them happy, and for which they strive. In each case, attaining these things might also make a person unhappy. For each item, list people that would be able to tell you how attaining it could make you unhappy. In other words, if you wanted to find out how attaining money could make you unhappy, who would you ask?

a) Money

b) Honor

c) Power

d) Fame

e) Pleasure

Writing Assignment 22

1. Pick one of the items from the list above and write a paragraph in your notebook explaining how having it could make you unhappy. Your paragraph should be written as if you are the person from whom you would seek to learn for that item. For example, if you said you wanted to ask a politician about the negative effects of power, write as if you are a politician.

2. Write an opening question for the discussion on the Consolation of Philosophy.

The Consolation of Philosophy
Boethius

Most people believe that money, honor, power, or pleasure will make them happy. Let me show you briefly how each one of these has something evil within itself. If you try to get money, you need to worry about keeping it, and must take more and more from others. If you receive honor from others, you owe a debt to those who give it to you. If you want more honor, you have to beg for it. If you get power, you risk being betrayed by those over whom you have power. If you seek fame, you lose your security and become involved in endless problems. If you seek a life of pleasure, you become dependent on the health of a weak and fragile thing—your body. For you're neither bigger than an elephant, nor stronger than a bull, nor faster than a tiger, and their bodies wear away.

Look up at the stars, and consider the size and the stability of the heavens, and stop admiring base things. Your own beauty passes away swiftly, even faster than that of the spring flowers. If we had eyes that could see through stone walls, wouldn't we find a beautiful body ugly when we saw the stomach, the liver, and all our insides? So it is not your own nature that makes you look beautiful, but the weak eyes of the other people who look at you. Admire your body as much as you like, but remember that what you admire so much can be destroyed by a slight fever that lasts only a few days.

All these arguments can be summed up in one truth: Money, honor, power, and pleasure are all limited. They make us believe they will make us happy, but they can't give happiness to us.

What incredible ignorance drives miserable men along these crooked paths! You don't look for gold in trees or for jewels growing on bushes. If you want a fish for dinner, you don't cast your nets up in high mountains. If you want to hunt deer, you don't go to the ocean. No, we are skilled in knowing the hidden caves in the sea; we know where pearls and precious gems are found. We know which lakes and waters have which fish. But when it comes to looking for the good that everyone wants, people are blind and ignorant. They look in places where they should know they will never find happiness. What can I say to show them what fools they are? Let them seek money, honor, power, fame, and pleasure. When they have painfully gotten what they wanted, they may finally see their mistake and learn that these goods are all false.

Possible Questions to Raise

- Which of the following would most likely make you happy: money, fame, power, pleasure, or honor?
- What other things might make someone happy?
- How might money (or honor, fame, power, pleasure) make you unhappy?
- What does Boethius mean by pleasure?
- What does Boethius mean by happiness?
- What other words might you use in place of happiness, in the way Boethius means happiness?

Exploring All Sides of an Issue

Students will explore the issue of factions from multiple perspectives and as it arises in various settings. They will also try to problem-solve concerning that issue within the settings they examine, and compare their solutions to those offered by James Madison in the Federalist Papers.

We all encounter factions. In fact, whenever we must work with others, factions are likely to arise. In students' previous experience with Touchstones, they have actively looked at how factions formed within a discussion group. The issue raises many questions: Why do factions occur? Are they useful or harmful? Can they be removed? If so, how? If they cannot be removed, then what should be done to minimize their negative effects?

The class will complete both the Individual Work and the Small Group Work before reading the text, *Federalist Paper 10*, by James Madison. Madison's argument covers many aspects of the issue of factions in the United States, from the causes to the corrections as well as the importance of dealing with this issue. He describes two solutions. The first is to remove the causes of factions; and the second is to make sure that everyone agrees. He promptly shows that to implement the first solution is to destroy freedom, and the second is impossible. The resulting conclusion is that factions are inevitable, and what must be considered is how to minimize the problems factions cause. He then outlines the differences between a "pure democracy" and a republic and says that it is in the form of a republic that the problem of factions can best be dealt with since a republic has chosen representatives who will filter the opinions of the masses and will be more likely to see beyond temporary concerns for the sake of the country.

In the discussion, students can explore all aspects of Madison's argument. It will be useful for them to explore whether there are any other cures that Madison does not discuss. Also, looking back at the Individual and Small Group Work and comparing the students' answers to those of Madison will give them an opportunity to further compare ideas and explore how different settings change both the problems and solutions to factions.

In Writing Assignment 23, the students are to agree or disagree with a quote from the text and to support whatever stance they take. This will help students practice constructing arguments, thinking critically, and supporting their opinions with reason and evidence.

Lesson Plan 23

1. SMALL GROUP WORK...10 minutes
   - Divide the class into four groups.
   - Have students compare their answers to question 2 from Worksheet 23 regarding ways to remove factions from various settings 1) a discussion group, 2) a classroom, 3) in government, or 4) among coworkers.
   - Have the students agree on one method for each setting.

2. GROUP REPORTS...10 minutes
   - Have each group report one of their solutions and compare their solution to other groups' ideas by asking whether or not other groups think each solution will work. A different small group should report on each of the different settings.

3. TEXT...3 minutes
   - Read the text aloud and have the students read it again silently.

4. OPENING QUESTIONS..3 minutes
   - Have students write down opening questions.

5. DISCUSSION..18 minutes
   - Begin with a student's question. You may want to bring up examples of factions in America today, whether they are good or bad, and what can or should be done to change them.

6. DISTRIBUTE WRITING ASSIGNMENTS..1 minute
   - Distribute Writing Assignment and Worksheet 24

Total: 45 minutes

Worksheet 23

1. Any time large numbers of people get together there will be different smaller groups of people with similar interests and beliefs, or factions. What are the ways in which factions can be good and bad?

   List a few ways in which factions might be good.

   List a few ways in which factions might be bad.

2. The following is a list of groups that may be made up of various factions. For each of them, come up with a few strategies you could use to remove factions or to get people from different factions to work cooperatively.

   A discussion group:

   A classroom:

   A government:

   A group of co-workers:

3. Write an opening question for the discussion on The Federalist Paper 10.

Writing Assignment 23

The following statement is an excerpt from the reading for today's class. Choose a stance toward the following statement (you can agree with it, disagree with it, or agree with some parts and disagree with others) and write an argument supporting your opinion with examples or reasons.

"The energy that produces different opinions concerning religion, government and many other points, and makes us follow different leaders—that same energy divides human beings into factions. It inflames them to dislike and hate one another."

The Federalist Papers 10
James Madison

Among the many advantages of a well-formed Union of all the States, none deserves more attention than its tendency to control violence among factions. By a faction I mean a number of citizens—either a majority of them or a minority of them—who group themselves together, and who are motivated by some common interest or cause. But this common interest or cause is opposed to and threatens the rights of other citizens, or the interests of the community as a whole.

There are two ways of removing the causes of faction. One of them is by destroying the freedom that is essential for faction to exist in the first place. The other way is to make sure that every citizen has the same opinions, the same passions, and the same interests.

Nothing is more true than that the first cure—to destroy the freedom of everyone—is far worse than the disease; that is, factions fighting each other. Liberty is to faction as air is to fire. But it would be as foolish to destroy liberty, which is essential to healthy political life, as it would be to destroy air, which is necessary for any animal life, simply because it also allows fire to exist.

The second cure—to make sure every citizen has the same opinions—is impossible. As long as the reason of human beings continues to make mistakes sometimes, and people are free to use their reason, there will be different opinions on all kinds of matters. As long as the connection continues between one's reason and self-love, they will constantly affect each other.

So, that which lies behind the causes of faction is part of the very nature of mankind. The energy that produces different opinions concerning religion, government, and many other points, and which makes us follow different leaders—that same energy divides human beings into factions. It inflames them to dislike and hate one another. It makes them much more likely to oppress and fight one another than to work for their common good.

It is because of the energy of this self-love and self-interest that no one is allowed to be a judge in one's own cause. It is even more certain that a group of people—a faction—should not be lawmakers, judge, and jury in their own cause at the same time.

From this it follows that a pure democracy, by which I mean a small society of people who try to govern themselves in person, will never cure the evils of faction. The majority will always rule over, and oppress, the minority. But a republic, by which I mean a government in which a scheme of representation takes place, promises a cure we are looking for.

The two main differences between a democracy and a republic are: first, that in a republic, the government is a small number of citizens elected by all the citizens; secondly, a republic can extend over a very large country and very many citizens.

The effect of these differences is that the many different opinions of the masses from all over the country will be refined by passing them through the medium of the representatives, chosen by all the citizens. These representatives are more likely to be wise enough to see better the true interest of their country, and less likely to sacrifice it to some temporary considerations.

In the next place, in a large republic, each representative will be chosen by a large number of citizens, and so it will be more difficult for unworthy candidates to cheat at getting elected.

Again, since the people are more free, they will be more likely to elect a person of attractive and stable character.

Possible Questions to Raise

- What are examples of factions in America today?
- Are there other cures for factions that Madison doesn't discuss?
- What are the differences between a democracy and a republic?
- Are factions inevitable?
- Why do factions exist?
- Do you think Madison's description of how a republic lessens the problem of factions is true? Has it worked in our country?

Learning Alone and Learning With Others

Students will explore two different media: a selection from Shakespeare and a painting. They will examine the differences between learning alone and learning with others, as well as how our expectations change the way we view a painting or read a text, and how these expectations can change the way we listen to others.

Lesson 24 has a variety of components related to teaching oneself. Using a painting and an excerpt from a play that each address being in prison, students will have the chance to look at 1) being alone versus being with others, 2) how different media affect the way we experience an idea, and 3) how our expectations change the way we view or understand something. But they will also practice teaching themselves by engaging with the painting through their writing assignment.

In Lesson 22, students discussed how to know when they can learn from others. In Lesson 24, they will look at the idea of learning with others. In the excerpt from *Richard II*, a few short lines emphasize the solitude of being in prison. Käthe Kollwitz's painting shows three prisoners listening to music together. While the students will not analyze the differences between these two "texts," they will have the opportunity to discuss how the experience of being in prison is different when one is alone than it is when one is with others, and when it would be better to learn something alone or to learn it along with others. Worksheet 24 presents students with two lists: one of things we learn, and one of situations. For each list they will be asked to decide whether they would rather be alone or with others. This choice will also be the focus of the discussion, which will start the class, rather than follow the small group work as in previous lessons.

When we read a text, we often try to recognize what the text can teach us. For most of us, most texts represent a mere source of information, and nothing more. In order to be active learners, we must learn to engage the text, question what it says, contrast it with our own beliefs, and resist the temptation to passively ingest what it says. Here paintings offer us a unique tool. Students often feel freer in exploring a painting, since there is less expectation of expertise and everyone feels equally legitimate in putting forth their own impressions and interpretations. Writing Assignment 24 and the Small Group Work focus on this freedom.

Writing Assignment 24 asks students to choose a single adjective to describe the painting and to support that choice with an argument. The exercise encourages the students to engage the painting actively and practice constructing an argument. In small groups, the students must decide how the title, which tells us that the men in the painting are prisoners, affects the way we view the painting. Writing Assignment 24 can be a useful contrast to the ideas that the small groups put forth concerning how we would have viewed the painting differently; what adjectives would they choose if the people in the painting were not prisoners?

This movement, from examining the painting alone to exploring it with others, will give students the experience of the differences between learning alone and learning with others. After the small groups report, you might address this explicitly with the students and see what differences they noticed between the two activities.

Lesson Plan 24

1. TEXT...3 minutes
   - The students will have read the text and seen the painting before class.
   - Have them read the text again silently, and give them a minute to look over the painting.

2. DISCUSSION...18 minutes
   - Randomly choose a student to pose the opening question.

3. SMALL GROUP WORK...8 minutes
   - Divide the class into groups of four or five.
   - Since the title of the painting lets them know they are looking at prisoners, have the students decide how knowing that they are prisoners affects how they imagine the scene.

4. GROUP REPORTS...15 minutes
   - Have each group report their conclusions.
   - Ask each group follow-up questions and encourage comparison between groups.
   - Ask the students about the differences between answering questions about the painting alone, as in Writing Assignment 24, and with others in the small groups.
   - If there is time, review the answers in the Individual Work about learning alone and with others. You may want to see if anyone has changed their mind.

5. DISTRIBUTE WRITING ASSIGNMENT...1minute
   - Distribute Writing Assignment and Worksheet 25

Total: 45 minutes

Worksheet 24

Students will need to have the text and the painting available to them to complete Worksheet 24.

1. The following is a list of things that people try to learn. For each, decide whether it would be easier to learn by yourself or with others.

	Better alone	Better with others
Painting	_____	_____
Reading	_____	_____
Mathematics	_____	_____
Playing the piano	_____	_____
Philosophy	_____	_____
Chemistry	_____	_____

2. Pick one of the items you thought would be better alone and one that you thought would be better with others and explain why.

Better alone:

Better with others:

3. Imagine that you are doing the following things. Decide whether it would be better to do them alone or with others.

	Better alone	Better with others
Listening to music	_____	_____
Examining a painting	_____	_____
Conducting scientific experiments	_____	_____
Interviewing an author	_____	_____
Being in prison	_____	_____

4. Write down an opening question for the discussion.

Writing Assignment 24

Think of one, and only one, adjective that best describes the painting, Prisoners Listening to Music, and write a paragraph explaining why you choose that adjective.

Richard II
William Shakespeare

King Richard II is a prisoner in Pomfret Castle.

> *Richard:*
> "I have been studying how I may compare
> This prison where I live unto the world.
> And, for because the world is populous,
> And here is not a creature but myself,
> I cannot do it.
> Yet I'll hammer it out."

Prisoners Listening to Music
Käthe Kollwitz

Possible Questions to Raise

- Which better portrays prison—the text or the painting?
- Would you rather be the king in the tower or one of the prisoners from the painting?
- What else might the prisoners be doing, other than listening to music?
- If they were not prisoners, who else might the people in the painting be?
- What are the differences between reading about something and seeing a painting of it? Is one better than the other?
- What would be the differences between being in prison alone and being with others? Which would you prefer?
- What might the king from the text go on to say after, "yet I'll hammer it out"?

Authority and Individuals

Students will explore when to obey the wishes of a leader or authority figure and when they should decide for themselves. They will respond to various situations in which one must make this decision and practice forming a counter argument to an author's opinion.

As we become independent thinkers, we encounter times when our own judgment runs counter to that of the people who have authority over us. Deciding what is our own responsibility and whether or not we should follow the decisions of these authority figures will be the topic of today's session. Throughout the year in Touchstones, students have taken various degrees of responsibility for the success of the discussion—whether through improving the focus of the group on the task, supplying questions and avenues for discussion, or simply moderating their own behavior to make room for others. In this way, everyone in the discussion is simultaneously a participant and a leader. And these two roles can conflict; a student may feel that for the good of the group he or she should let someone else speak while simultaneously wanting to respond or ask a question to satisfy their own interests.

In *A Theological-Political Treatise*, by Benedict de Spinoza, the leader is external. Spinoza describes a conflict between acting for the good of the state or government and acting according to other duties, even moral ones. According to Spinoza, the duty to our government is the highest duty and overrules all others. While a person may feel it is his or her duty to offer assistance to a condemned man, for example, no one should offer any help. Spinoza bases this on the statement that without government, there would only be anarchy and that that is the worst fate. Therefore, everything we do must "preserve" the state for the good of everyone. He goes so far as to say that this "good of all the people is the supreme principle to which all other laws—divine and human—must be secondary" and that the ruler is the interpreter of religion because it is the ruler that decides how we act toward our neighbor. The presence of divine law in the text also makes it possible for students to look at the conflict as one between two external leaders.

In the Individual Work, the students are asked to choose between following a leader's rule or deciding for themselves in terms of their education—what they study or for how long. The second part of the worksheet asks students to imagine situations in which what they think is right as individuals might go against the will of their leaders or the good of more people. Students will have spent some time exploring the issue on their own before coming to class. Writing Assignment 25 will continue this examination by having the students write an argument agreeing or disagreeing with a statement from the text, "It is certain a man's duties to his country are the highest he can fulfill." As with past lessons, the students will spend some time teaching themselves about the topic and then compare their ideas with those of their classmates and of the author.

After reading the text, the students will work in small groups to write a paragraph or two arguing against Spinoza's claims. Worksheet and Writing Assignment 25 will have prepared them to counter Spinoza, and the groups should first compare their answers to question 2 on Worksheet 25.

Lesson Plan 25

1. TEXT..2 minutes
   - Read the text aloud and have students read it again silently.

2. OPENING QUESTIONS...2 minutes
   - Have students write opening questions on their worksheets.

3. SMALL GROUP WORK..12 minutes
   - Divide the class into groups of four or five.
   - Have the groups rephrase Spinoza's argument in a paragraph or two. Have them compare their answers to question 2 since the situations described might help them provide reasons or examples for use in their counter argument. Some students may have taken a similar stance in Writing Assignment 25 and should feel free to apply that.

4. GROUP REPORTS..10 minutes
   - Have each group read their summary and then ask how the summaries differed.

5. DISCUSSION..18 minutes
   - Randomly select a student to ask the opening question. One important topic will be whether rulers can or should decide how people should behave. Mention different examples of people one might behaving toward (i.e. neighbors, family, or strangers).

6. DISTRIBUTE WRITING ASSIGNMENT...1 minute
   - Distribute Writing Assignment and Worksheet 26.
   - Students will need to take the text home with them to complete the assignments.

Total: 45 minutes

Worksheet 25

1. There are many things that should be decided by an authority and many that should be decided by individuals. For each of the decisions below, who should make the decision— the individual or an authority figure like a teacher, parent, or government leader?

	Authority Figure	Individual
What subjects to study	_____	_____
What books to read	_____	_____
How to treat other people	_____	_____
What time to be home	_____	_____

2. Sometimes the things that individual people want turn out to be bad for the community as a whole. For each of the following communities, think of something an individual might want to do that would be bad for the community as a whole. For example, in a class at school, a student might want to listen to loud music, but that would prevent the rest of the students from being able to hear one another or concentrate on their work.

In school:

In a neighborhood:

In a country:

In a discussion group:

Writing Assignment 25

1. The following statement is an excerpt from the reading for today's class. Choose a stance toward the following statement (you can agree with it, disagree with it, or agree with some parts and disagree with others) and write an argument supporting your opinion.

   "It is certain a man's duties to his country are the highest he can fulfill."

   For whatever stance you choose, compare duties to one's country to other duties.

2. Write an opening question for the discussion on A Theological-Political Treatise.

A Theological-Political Treatise
Benedict de Spinoza

It is certain that a man's duties to his country are the highest he can fulfill. For if government be taken away, nothing good can last. Without government, everything becomes open to dispute and argument. Anger and anarchy are unchecked and there is universal fear. So there can be no external and public duty toward our neighbor that would not become a crime if it involved injury to the state. Nor can there be any violation of our duty to our neighbor in anything we do for the sake of preserving the state.

For example, in the abstract, it is my duty when my neighbor quarrels with me and wishes to steal my jacket, to give him my coat too. But if it is thought that such actions are harmful to the maintenance of the state, I should bring my neighbor to trial even at the risk of his being punished by death. This is why the ancient Roman Manlius Torquatus was held in such great honor when he showed that his duty toward the state was more important to him even than his duty toward his children. The good of all the people is the supreme principle to which all other laws—both Divine and human—must be secondary.

It is the function of the ruler alone to decide what is necessary for the public good and for the safety of the state. Therefore, it is also the ruler's role, whether a king or a legislature rules a country, to decide the limits of our duty toward our neighbor. In other words, the ruler must determine how we should obey God in outward actions though not in the thoughts that are private to each of us. We can now see in what way the ruler is the interpreter of religion. For no one can obey God rightly if his obedience does not support the public good. So each person must implicitly obey all the ruler's commands. By God's command, we are bound to do our duty to all men without any exception, and to injure no one. We also have a duty not to help one person through another person's injury or loss, much less at a loss to the whole state. Now, no private citizen can judge what is good for the whole state. Private citizens learn what is good from the ruler whose right it is to deal with all public affairs. So no one can rightly practice piety or obedience to God unless he obeys the ruler's commands in all public things. This is shown to be true also by our experience. If a ruler judges someone to be worthy of death, imprisonment, or to be considered an enemy—whether that person be a citizen or a foreigner, a private individual, or himself a ruler—no citizen is allowed to give the condemned person assistance.

Possible Questions to Raise

- Should a ruler decide how we treat one another? Should someone other than a ruler decide?
- What duties might conflict with our duties to our country?
- Why does Spinoza think that duty to one's country is most important?
- Where do we learn right and wrong? Who decides?
- Should you get to decide for yourself what you study in school?
- What parts of your life should be your decision and not that of others?

Learning from Foreign Texts

Students will practice teaching themselves by examining a text from a foreign culture and attempting to put certain ideas into their own words. The group has spent a good deal of time this year exploring their fundamental beliefs and assumptions, sometimes directly and sometimes indirectly. Texts from foreign cultures can be a unique tool for continuing this exercise. Because the concepts and ideas come from a different set of assumptions and cultural influences, these texts offer us a chance to compare and contrast, to make ours more visible and capable of being examined. While past sessions have done much of this exploration through the discussion, today students will first do it themselves by trying to put concepts and ideas that may seem odd to them into their own words.

The text for Lesson 26 is from the *Bhagavad-Gita*. In it, a famous warrior asks Krishna how to justify going to war when prayer is considered the superior life. Krishna's answer is full of ideas that may be very easily understood by Eastern cultures, but not so easily understood from a Western perspective. He describes prayer as true knowledge, prayer in the shape of action, and action as a type of sacrifice. While the words "prayer," "action," and "sacrifice" are familiar to us, they do not seem to have the same meaning in this text. This text provides an opportunity to translate foreign ideas into our own understanding, and thereby offers the students a chance to explore how they can learn from other cultures.

The students will read the text before completing Worksheet 26. The worksheet asks them to rewrite some of the phrases from the text in their own words. Because the concepts themselves are foreign, this will be more than trying to find synonyms for action, prayer, and sacrifice—it will force the students to attempt to bridge the gap between different cultures. The small groups will continue this effort as the students compare their translations and come up with a single translation on which they agree. The students will then examine the process of translating, and how each of their processes differs from those of their classmates. These differences should be the topic of the group reports. Instead of reporting in turn, ask the entire class whether translating is easier on their own or with others. This question explicitly addresses the theme we have examined in Lessons 22 through 24—learning by yourself and with others. Ask whether any of the translations are significantly different, and explore why they might vary so much. Because Writing Assignment 26 asked the students to assume that action could be sacrifice and to explain how that is true, it will be a further opportunity to compare their responses to the text.

Comparing different cultures will be an important topic during the discussion and you may choose to approach it from a variety of angles. Questions about what people can learn from other cultures, what ideas from our culture would be difficult for others to understand, and what in our own culture is similar to the ideas in the text may all prove to be fruitful starting points for this discussion.

Lesson Plan 26

1. TEXT..3 minutes
   - Read the text aloud and have the students read it again silently.

2. OPENING QUESTIONS..3 minutes
   - Have the students write opening questions on Worksheet 26.

3. SMALL GROUP WORK..10 minutes
   - Have the groups compare their answers from Worksheet 26 and decide upon a single translation for each phrase or sentence.

4. GROUP REPORTS..10 minutes
   - Ask the entire class whether the translation exercise was easier to do alone or in their small groups.
   - Ask if any of the groups have examples where their answers were very different.

5. DISCUSSION...18 minutes
   - Randomly select a student to ask the opening question.
   - *Note:* Possible topics may include what we can learn from other societies, the life of prayer versus the life of action, and whether you can free yourself from worldly attachments and cultural ideas.

6. DISTRIBUTE WRITING ASSIGNMENT..1 minute
   - Distribute Writing Assignment and Worksheet 27.

Total: 45 minutes

Worksheet 26

The Bhagavad-Gita comes from another culture and presents several ideas and views in ways that may be unfamiliar to us.

1. Read the text before completing Worksheet and Writing Assignment 26.

2. Each of the following is a phrase or sentence from the text. Rewrite each of them in your own words.

   a) "The life of prayer is superior to the life of action"

   b) "prayer in the form of true knowledge"

   c) "prayer in the form of action"

   d) "You must act in order to live."

   e) "He…who learns not to think about worldly treasures, who frees himself from worldly attachments, and then, offering himself as a sacrifice, acts, is superior."

Writing Assignment 26

1. In a paragraph or two, describe how action can be sacrifice. Support your opinion with either the text or examples.

2. Write an opening question for the discussion on the Bhagavad-Gita.

The Bhagavad-Gita

The great warrior Arjuna said:

If, O lord Krishna, you consider that the life of prayer is superior to the life of action, why do you urge me to go to war, which is the most fearful action of all? Why do you confuse me by saying two things at once? Say one thing definitely so I will know how to gain the greatest good.

The lord Krishna replied:

O man without fault, I have already said that in this world there are two true paths: that of prayer in the form of true knowledge, and that of prayer in the shape of action. A man does not attain freedom from action merely by not acting. He does not attain perfection by simply giving up all worldly treasures. Nobody can live, even for an instant, without performing some action.

The man who keeps himself from acting, even though he is always thinking about worldly treasures, is fooling himself. Such a man is called a hypocrite. But he, O Arjuna, who learns not to think about worldly treasures, who frees himself from worldly attachments, and then, offering himself as a sacrifice, acts, is superior.

You should perform the actions that your duty as a warrior requires you to perform. For sacrificial action is better than inaction. You must act in order to live. All actions do indeed chain you to this world, except the action that is performed as a sacrifice. So, you must perform your actions as sacrifices if you are to break your attachments to the material world.

Possible Questions to Raise

- Was it easier to translate alone or with others?
- How can action be sacrifice?
- What types of things can we learn from other cultures?
- What ideas or beliefs from our culture might be difficult for people from other cultures to understand?
- How diverse is our discussion group?
- Does everyone in our discussion group share the exact same culture? Why?
- How can prayer be in the form of action?
- How is the "life of prayer" in the text different from what we might mean by that?
- Can you free yourself from worldly attachments?
- Is it possible to change the ideas and beliefs that you gain from your culture?

Inherited Opinions

Using a text that discusses the difference between opinions and prejudices, students will explore how many of our ideas are inherited and what we can do to challenge and even change them. To be able to teach oneself effectively requires that we be able to examine all of our ideas and beliefs, and that we have the skills needed to step back and view them from a distance. Many of our beliefs are not even our own, they are inherited from our culture, our friends, the media, and our families. Perhaps having heard them enough times we start to think they are our own, or at the least, we never stop to question their validity.

In *The Rights of Women*, Mary Wollstonecraft describes how people are often content to accept the thoughts of others, rather than exercising their own minds. When these thoughts come from people who are respected, their ideas are adopted with great vehemence. Wollstonecraft goes on to describe how prejudices often begin as opinions that are based upon some evidence and relevant to a specific time or circumstance. Yet when these opinions become lazily accepted outside of the particular circumstance of their origin, they turn into prejudices, and people are unwilling, even unable, to justify them beyond saying they are true "just because." Finally, she discusses how one might re-examine his or her prejudices. And while her solution is to go back to the principles that preceded the prejudices, she admits that this strategy will often fail, since the listener does not wish to have any doubts about such strongly held ideas. Wollstonecraft's solution is similar to the students' efforts to reconsider their fundamental beliefs. In Lesson 27, the class will move beyond examining the idea to examine the act of reconsideration itself.

Worksheet 27 asks them to identify the sources of prejudice. A second question asks them to decide whether a certain set of prejudices are more likely to be opinions that a person forms for him or herself, or ideas that have been received from others. Writing Assignment 27 continues this idea and asks students to deal with exactly the same issue as the text, by asking them to write a paragraph describing the difference between opinions and prejudices.

Lesson Plan 27

1. TEXT..3 minutes
   - Read the text aloud and have the students read it again silently.

2. OPENING QUESTIONS...3 minutes
   - Have all students write an opening question for the discussion.

3. DISCUSSION..23 minutes
   - Randomly select a student to ask the opening question.

4. SMALL GROUP WORK...5 minutes
   - Divide the class into groups of four or five. Groups are to try and decide the best way to help someone overcome prejudices.

5. GROUP REPORTS...10 minutes
   - Have groups report their decisions and encourage discussion between groups. Ask follow-up questions and ask other groups to comment on the reports

6. DISTRIBUTE WRITING ASSIGNMENT...1 minute
   - Distribute Writing Assignment and Worksheet 28.

Total: 45 minutes

Worksheet 27

1. Rank the following items from 1 to 5, where 1 is the source of the most prejudices and 5 is the source of the least prejudices.

_____ Friends

_____ Family

_____ Oneself

_____ Society

_____ TV/Media

2. Which of the following decisions do you think people decide for themselves and which do you think are ideas or decisions received from others? On a scale of 1 to 10 rate each decision. (A 1 represents something that people usually decide for themselves, and a 10 represents something that is usually received from others.)

	Self									**Others**
What religion to be a part of	1	2	3	4	5	6	7	8	9	10
What career to go into	1	2	3	4	5	6	7	8	9	10
Who to be friends with	1	2	3	4	5	6	7	8	9	10
How to treat other people	1	2	3	4	5	6	7	8	9	10
What activities or hobbies to do	1	2	3	4	5	6	7	8	9	10

Writing Assignment 27

1. In your notebook, describe the difference between opinions and prejudices in one paragraph.

2. Write an opening question for the discussion on *The Rights of Women*.

The Rights of Women
Mary Wollstonecraft

Mental activity, like bodily activity, is at first difficult and unpleasant. Therefore, many people let others both work and think for them. When in a group, a person asserts an opinion with great heat, very often it is a prejudice. Generally such a person has a high respect for the understanding of some relative or friend without fully understanding the opinions that he is now so eager to have us also believe. Therefore, he holds these opinions with a degree of force that would surprise even the person who held them in the first place.

It is now fashionable to respect prejudices. When we dare to face our prejudices, motivated by feelings of humanity and armed with reason, we are often asked whether our ancestors, who created these opinions, were fools. I reply that they weren't. Our ancestors' opinions were all probably thought about and based on some reason. But often the reason they had was special and useful only at that time. It was not a fundamental principle that would be reasonable at all times.

Our ancestors' old and moss-covered opinions become prejudices when we lazily accept them only because these opinions have been with us for a long time. An opinion is a prejudice when it is one that we like and hold strongly, but for which we can give no reason. The moment a reason can be given for an opinion, it stops being a prejudice, though it may still be a mistake or an error. This way of arguing, if we can call it arguing, reminds me of what is crudely and vulgarly called "a woman's reason." For women sometimes say they love someone or believe certain things just because they love or believe them, and they can't or won't give any reasons.

It is useless to talk with people who only use affirmatives and negatives, who say either "yes" or "no" to everything. Before you can bring yourself or someone else to a point where you can begin a useful discussion, you must go back to the simple principles that precede the prejudices. And it is ten to one that you will be stopped as you try to do this. You even will be told that, though these simple principles are true in theory, they are false in practice. When you hear this from people, you may infer that their reason has whispered some doubts to them. For it generally happens that people assert their opinions with the greatest heat when they begin to waver and have doubts about them. They then try to drive out their own doubts by convincing their opponents, and grow angry when their own doubts continue to bother and haunt them.

Possible Questions to Raise

- Where do opinions come from?
- How can you tell the difference between your own opinions and the ones you inherit from others?
- What are some personal examples of changing prejudices? How did it happen?
- What does Wollstonecraft think is the difference between an opinion and a prejudice?
- Should prejudices be respected?
- How does an opinion become a prejudice?

Engaging the Text

Students will examine the various aspects of a piece of fiction, looking at the style, content, imagery, and how they work together to achieve meaning. They will engage the reading by both continuing the story and looking at how it could be different. Reading actively is an important aspect of being an active and engaged learner. The exercises in Lesson 28 are chosen to help students practice reading actively. Making conscious the many things we do as we read, identifying the choices that the author has made, co-imagining with the author as we read, anticipating what will come next, whether we are right or wrong, are all responsibilities of an active reader. These responsibilities are ours and wondering whether we are reading a piece of fiction, a philosophical argument, or even a mathematical proof.

The text, from *Almos' a Man* by Richard Wright, is a piece of fiction that is in many ways unclear about what is happening or why. The voice of the only character is also written in dialect, which further estranges us from the story. The story relates a sequence of events that a man named Dave Sanders goes through, all of which are related to his idea of being or becoming a man. He digs up a gun that he has buried and then works up the courage to shoot it, with his eyes open. There is a paragraph in which he debates shooting it at another man's house in order to prove his manhood. Finally, he awaits a train that is passing and manages to jump up onto the train, heading for "somewhere he could be a man."

The students are asked to engage this text in several ways. First, they are asked to identify the elements that are related to the title, the images or events that have something to do with manhood. They will also be asked to imagine how the story might be different if instead of a man, it was a woman. And finally, in their writing assignment, they will be asked to continue the story, to imagine what happens next.

In Lesson 24, we had the students engage the painting entitled, Prisoners Listening to Music. Both fiction and paintings offer a unique type of text for helping students engage the text. When we read non-fiction, it is very easy for us to take on a passive role, to assume that the text has something to impart to us and we are merely the recipients of information. We do not question the text except to ask what it has to offer us. But with paintings and fiction, we often feel as readers or viewers that we have more freedom to interpret what we read or see. Our own role in the activity of reading becomes more important. In Touchstones, we want to encourage this same level of activity with everything we read. We interact with the text, compare it to our own opinions and experiences, question it, and investigate its claims.

In the Small Group Work, each student should read their paragraphs and, as a group, decide upon a single one. The group may select one student's paragraph, or create a composite of several students' paragraphs. When they report, they should read the group's version aloud. Prompt the discussion by asking what style, elements, or characteristics of the Richard Wright story they were trying to maintain.

Lesson Plan 28

1. SMALL GROUP WORK...13 minutes
   - Divide the class into groups of four or five.
   - Have the students compare their writing assignments and decide between their versions or create some composite. Tell them they will be asked to explain their choice.

2. GROUP REPORTS..10 minutes
   - Ask the groups follow-up questions regarding what elements, style, or characteristics of the story they decided to represent in their paragraphs.

3. TEXT..3 minutes
   - Read the text aloud and have students read it again silently.

4. DISCUSSION..18 minutes
   - Randomly select a student to ask the opening question.

5. DISTRIBUTE WRITING ASSIGNMENT...1 minute
   - Distribute Writing Assignment and Worksheet 29.

Total: 45 minutes

Worksheet 28

Read the text before completing Worksheet and Writing Assignment 28.

1. Identify the images or events in the text that relate to the title, Almos' a Man.

2. How would the story be different if it was Almos' a Woman? You may want to see how it would change the items you listed above.

3. Write an opening question on the text for your group to discuss.

Writing Assignment 28

Write two more paragraphs for the story. In other words, imagine what happens next. Do not be too concerned with imitating the author's style. You will compare your paragraphs with the paragraphs of the other students in class.

Almos' a Man
Richard Wright

The moon was bright. He ran almost all the way to the edge of the woods. He stumbled over the ground, looking for the spot where he had buried the gun. Yeah, here it is. Like a hungry dog scratching for a bone he pawed it up. He puffed his black cheeks and blew dirt from the trigger and barrel. He broke it and found four cartridges unshot. He looked around; the fields were filled with silence and moonlight. He clutched the gun stiff and hard in his fingers. But as soon as he wanted to pull the trigger, he shut his eyes and turned his head. "Naw, Ah can't shoot wid mah eyes closed n mah head turned." With effort he held his eyes open; then he squeezed. Blooooom! Click, click. There! It was empty. If anybody could shoot a gun, he could. He put the gun into his hip pocket and started across the fields.

When he reached the top of a ridge he stood straight and proud in the moonlight, looking at Jim Hawkins' big white house, feeling the gun sagging in his pocket. "Lawd, ef Ah had jus one mo bullet Ahd taka shot at tha house. Ahd like t scare ol man Hawkins jussa little . . . Jussa enough t let im know Dave Sanders is a man."

To his left the road curved, running to the tracks of the Illinois Central. He jerked his head, listening. From far off came a faint hoooof-hoooof; hoooof-hoooof . . . That's number eight. He took a swift look at Jim Hawkins' white house; he thought of pa, of ma, of his little brother, and the boys. He thought of the dead mule and heard hoooof-hoooof; hoooof-hoooof; hoooof-hoooof ... He stood rigid. "Two dollahs a mont. Les see now... Tha means it ll take bout two years. Shucks! Ahll be dam!"

He started down the road, towards the tracks. Yeah, here she comes! He stood beside the track and held himself stiffly. "Here she comes, erroun the ben... C'mon, yuh slow poke! C'mon!" He had his hand on his gun; something quivered in his stomach. Then the train thundered past, the gray and brown boxcars rumbling and clinking. He gripped the gun tightly; then he jerked his hand out of his pocket. "Ah betcha Bill wouldn't do it! Ah betcha..." The cars slid past, steel grinding upon steel. "Ahm riding yuh ternight so hep me Gawd!" He was hot all over. He hesitated just a moment; then he grabbed, pulled atop of a car, and lay flat. He felt his pocket. The gun was still there. Ahead the long rails were glinting in moonlight, stretching away, away to somewhere, somewhere where he could be a man...

Possible Questions to Raise

- How would the story be different if it was entitled *Almos' a Woman*? Would anything be the same?
- Why does the author write the voice of the lead character in dialect?
- What images strike you as being most about manhood?
- Was this text easier to read or harder than others? Why?

Conflicting Perspectives

Often in this year's Touchstones classes, we have addressed the various perspectives that can be taken on any issue. In Lesson 29, students will examine how a single issue or problem can be good for one and bad for another, and the ways in which those opposing viewpoints interact.

Florence Nightingale, in *Cassandra*, makes plain the conflict that can come between two perspectives. The reading begins with the statement that suffering or pain is better than nothing, because out of suffering can come change. The argument goes on to show that what is painful to one, is usually beneficial to another.

For Nightingale, there are two classes, those who are born into benefit and those who are not. Out of the mixture, comes progress. Those who suffer, strive to change things, to make things better. Conversely, those who have the benefits make it possible to retain the good things. So both classes are necessary requirements for progress—one class to make sure things keep changing, while the other class makes sure that the beneficial aspects remain.

On Worksheet 29, the students are to make a list of three or four things that they think are problems in our society. They are then asked to imagine the other side and describe who might benefit from those problems and how. Writing Assignment 29 will ask them to make an argument related to a statement pulled from the text, which states that change comes from those who are discontented.

The Small Group Work has two parts. First, the students are to compare their answers to the first two questions—their lists of problems in society and how those problems could be good for some people. They decide upon a single list of four problems that they have identified. For each problem, they must decide whether the problem can be fixed in such a way as to make both sides happy. When the groups report, ask other groups to offer feedback on their solutions. If different groups have the same or similar problems, spend some time comparing their solutions.

After the Small Group Work and reports, have students volunteer the topics that they listed and write these on the board. During the discussion, you and the students can refer to this list to keep the discussion moving or to change topics.

Lesson Plan 29

1. TEXT...3 minutes
   - Read the text aloud and have the students read it again silently.

2. OPENING QUESTIONS...4 minutes
   - Have the students write an opening question for the discussion. They are also asked to write a list of topics to be discussed.

3. SMALL GROUP WORK..10 minutes
   - Divide the class into groups of four or five.
   - Have them compare their worksheets and come up with a list of four problems.
   - Have the students describe whether those problems can be solved in such a way as to make both sides happy.

4. GROUP REPORTS...10 minutes
   - Ask other groups if they agree or disagree with the proposed solutions.

5. STUDENT TOPICS..2 minutes
   - Have students volunteer the topics they thought should be discussed, write as many as you can on the board.

6. DISCUSSION...15 minutes
   - Randomly select a student to pose the opening question.
   - If the discussion lags, refer to the list of topics to help guide the discussion in new directions.
   - Share this responsibility with the students, asking which topics haven't been discussed, or if they have questions about any of the topics.

7. DISTRIBUTE WRITING ASSIGNMENT..1 minute
   - Distribute Writing Assignment and Worksheet 30.
   - Students will need a copy of the text for Lesson 30 in order to complete their worksheets and writing assignments.

Total: 45 minutes

Worksheet 29

1. Come up with a list of four or five things in our society that cause problems to some people.

2. For each item, describe how that problem could be a good thing for others.

Writing Assignment 29

1. The following statement is an excerpt from the reading for today's class. Choose a stance toward the following statement (you can agree with it, disagree with it, or agree with some parts and disagree with others) and write an argument supporting your opinion. Provide examples and reasons for your opinion.

   "Were no people discontented with what they have, the world would never change and reach anything better."

2. Write an opening question for the discussion on Cassandra.

Cassandra
Florence Nightingale

Give us back our suffering, suffering rather than indifference. For out of nothing comes nothing, but out of suffering may come a cure. Better to have pain than paralysis. A hundred people struggle and drown in the waves at the shore. One discovers the new world. Rather, ten times rather, die in the surf, showing the way to the new world, than stand idly by on the far shore.

Look at that lizard. "It is not hot," he says. "I like the heat. The temperature which destroys you is life to me." Similarly, the state of society, of which some complain, makes others happy. Why should those who suffer complain to those who are happy? The happy do not suffer. They would not understand the complaints any more than the lizard would understand the sufferings of a sheep in the heat.

The changing world is necessarily divided into two classes. There are those who are born to the best of what there is and enjoy it. On the other hand, there are those who wish for something different and better, and try to create it. Without both these classes, the world would be badly off. Both classes are the very conditions of progress. Were no people discontented with what they have, the world would never change and reach anything better. And through the other class, a balance is secured. By enjoying the best of what is created, the good things that have been made are retained for the world. And we must not quarrel with either class for not possessing the privileges of the other. The laws of the nature of each make that impossible.

Is discontent and complaint a privilege? Yes, it is a privilege for you to suffer for your class—a privilege not reserved for the Redeemer and the martyrs alone. It is a privilege enjoyed by large numbers in every age. But the commonplace life of thousands has little interest because it is merely a common suffering. It is the story of those who do not have the courage either to fight against and resist or to accept the civilization of their time as the other classes do.

Possible Questions to Raise

- How does change happen in society?
- What is the difference between change and progress?
- Do you agree with Nightingale that both classes are needed for change?
- Quoting the text: "Are discontent and complaint a privilege?"
- Are there problems in society that are good for no one or are all good for some and bad for others?
- What does Nightingale mean by, "Rather, ten times rather, die in the surf, showing the way to the new world, than stand idly by on the far shore?"

Changing Beliefs

Students will look at the advantages and disadvantages that can come with changing one's beliefs. Throughout Touchstones, the students have continually examined belief structures and assumptions; they have assumed other perspectives and looked at how they may conflict. For this last class, the very topic of changing one's beliefs will be the focus of the discussion. We have been striving to enable your students to become capable of teaching themselves. This task includes all aspects of their beliefs as well as their habits. And while many, if not all of your students, may not have actually changed any of their fundamental beliefs, they will at least have been asked to look at them objectively and to compare them to those of others.

In Lesson 30, the question is whether one should change his or her own beliefs or those of others. What is lost when we change a belief? There is a stability in being certain of our beliefs that can be lost when we put them to question. In the text, *What is a Man?*, Mark Twain describes a man who is taken in by two different families when he is ill. In both cases, a young boy in the family is also ill. In the first case, the family is Christian and the man, thinking they are wrong to believe in God, changes the boy's mind. He succeeds but is struck when the dying boy and his mother chastise him for doing so. The man repents and comes to be a Christian himself. Later, as a missionary, another family takes him in. This time, he convinces a second dying boy to believe in his God rather than the multiple gods of the child's own faith. Again, he succeeds, but is again chastised by both the dying child and the mother.

The story is told in dialogue between an Old Man and a Young Man. At the end, the Young Man says that the man's conscience is a fool and that it doesn't know right from wrong. This statement will be the starting point for the students' work. Worksheet 30 has the students decide in both cases if the man was wrong in changing the boys' beliefs and to explain why or why not. This exercise lays the groundwork for discussing whether the righteousness of changing a belief depends on the righteousness of the belief, or whether it is damaging to change any belief, right or wrong.

Writing Assignment 30 refers to the last statement in the text. The statement can be understood in different ways and these differences will be a fruitful avenue for the discussion. For instance, does the Young Man feel that the man's conscience is a fool because he set about to change beliefs in general or because he was wrong in one case and right in another?

Lesson Plan 30

1. SMALL GROUP WORK...8 minutes
   - Divide the class into groups of four or five.
   - Have the students compare their answers to question 3 on the Worksheet 30.
   - Groups are to come up with ideas on how to change each belief.

2. GROUP REPORTS...12 minutes
   - Have each group report.
   - Ask other groups to comment on whether or not they think the solutions will work.
   - Ask: If the solution did work, what might the negative consequences be?

3. TEXT...4 minutes
   - Read the text aloud and have students read it again silently.

4. DISCUSSION..21 minutes
   - Randomly select a student to ask the opening question.
   - At some point, draw attention to the last line of the text, if the students have not already done so.
   - *Note:* Since this is the last Touchstones class, you may want to ask about beliefs and opinions that have changed during the discussions.

Total: 45 minutes

Worksheet 30

The man in the story convinces the two sick boys to change their beliefs. Decide whether he behaved wrongly with each.

1. Was he wrong when he convinced the first boy to give up his belief in one god?

    Yes   No

    Why?

2. Was he wrong when he convinced the second boy to believe in one god?

    Yes   No

    Why?

3. What is a belief that you think no one could convince you to change?

Writing Assignment 30

1. In today's reading, the Young Man who hears the story comments about the man in the story "The man's conscience was a fool. It didn't know right from wrong." Do you agree? Write a paragraph deciding whether or not the Young Man was right and explain your choice.

2. Write an opening question for the discussion on this text.

What is a Man?
Mark Twain

An *Old Man* is speaking to a *Young Man.*

Old Man: I will tell you a little story. Once upon a time an infidel, that is, a non-Christian, was a guest in the house of a Christian widow whose little boy was ill and near death. The non-Christian often watched by the bedside and entertained the boy with talk, and he used these opportunities to satisfy a strong longing of his own nature. He wanted other people to believe what he did, so he started to change the boy's opinions. He was successful. But the dying boy blamed him, and said, "I used to believe, and I was happy. You destroyed my belief and my comfort. Now I have nothing and I die miserable."

And the mother also blamed him and said, "My child is forever lost, and my heart is broken. How could you do such a cruel thing? We did you no harm. We made our house your home, and this is how you paid us."

The heart of the non-Christian was filled with sorrow for what he had done and he said, "It was wrong, but I was only trying to do him good. In my view he was in error, and it seemed my duty to teach him the truth."

Then the mother said, "I had taught him, all his little life, what I believed to be the truth, and in our faith we were both happy. Now he is dead and I am miserable. What right had you to disturb it? Where was your shame?"

Young Man: What a wicked man. He deserved death!

Old Man: He thought so himself, and said so.

Young Man: Ah, you see, his conscience was awakened!

Old Man: Perhaps. But what is clear is that it *hurt* him to see the mother suffer. At least, he was sorry he had done something that brought pain to himself. He had had so much pleasure while he had been changing the young boy's opinions he had forgotten the mother. He never realized that the mother's sorrow would bring pain to himself.

Young Man: How wonderful! The man's conscience was now awake. A cure like that is forever.

Old Man: Pardon. You should wait until I finish the story: The non-Christian was so filled with sorrow that he became quite changed about the little boy's religion. First, he became tolerant; next he looked at it fondly; and finally he began learning more and more about the boy's religion. From that moment, his progress was quick. He became a believing Christian. And he was so sorry for what he had done earlier that he became a missionary.

Later, while traveling through the world, he landed up ill and helpless in a faraway non-Christian country. A native widow took him into her home and nursed him back to health. Then her little son was taken ill, and the grateful missionary helped her care for him. Here was his first chance to make up for that terrible wrong he had done as a young man. He tried to persuade the little boy to give up his belief in false gods, and he was successful. But the dying boy blamed him, and said, "I used to believe in many gods, and I was happy. You destroyed my belief and my comfort. Now I have nothing and I die miserable."

And the mother also blamed him, and said, "My child is forever lost, and my heart is broken. How could you do such a cruel thing? We did you no harm. We made our house your home, and this is how you paid us."

The heart of the missionary was filled with sorrow for what he had done, and he said, "It was wrong, but I was only trying to do him good."

And the missionary's heart was filled with sorrow, and he was bitterly unhappy with himself just as in the earlier case. There! The story is finished. What is your comment?

Young Man: The man's conscience was a fool! It didn't know right from wrong.

Possible Questions to Raise

- What does the Young Man mean when he says, "[the man's conscience] didn't know right from wrong?"
- Should you change a deeply held belief? Even if it is wrong?
- What are some of the bad effects of changing beliefs? What are the good effects?
- Are there beliefs you could never change?
- Should the man in the story have changed either boy's beliefs?
- What is it that is painful about changing beliefs?
- Can a belief be neither right or wrong?
- What is the difference between changing a belief and changing an opinion or an idea?

LaVergne, TN USA
27 January 2010
171238LV00001B/18/A

9 781878 461711